GOING BACK TO CENTRAL

ON THE ROAD IN SEARCH OF THE PAST
IN MICHIGAN'S UPPER PENINSULA

Lon L. Emerick

Eagle Harbor

Eagle River

Central

Cliff ● ● Phoenix

Mohawk

Allouez ● ● Ahmeek

Copper City

Kearsarge

Gay

Calumet ● ● Laurium

Lake Linden

Hancock

Houghton

L a k e

Chassel

Askel Hill ●

Keweenaw Bay

Aura

Pequaming

Baraga

L'Anse

● Alberta

🦌 *Craig Lake*

Michigamme

Three Lakes ●

Champion

Lake Michigamme

Humbolt

Benchmark Associates, Inc.
Marquette, MI

Upper Peninsula
of Michigan

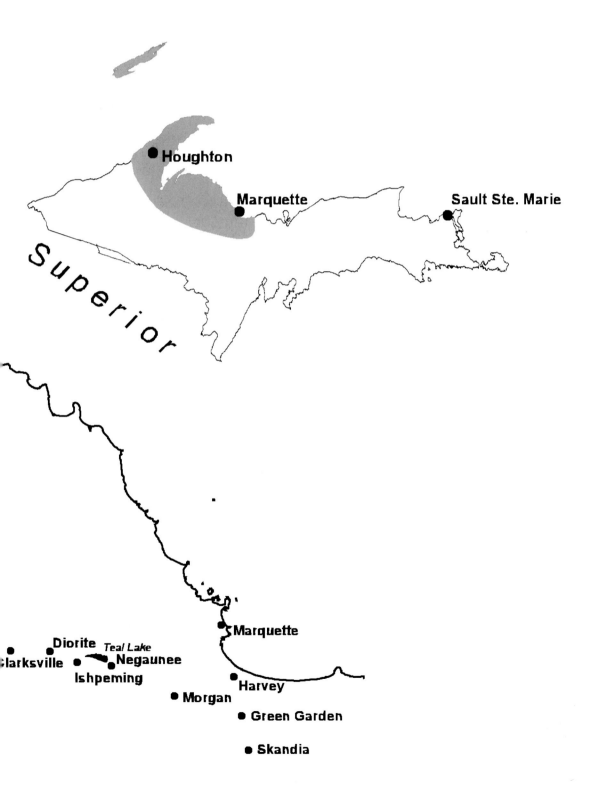

First Edition
All Rights Reserved

ISBN 096-50577-4-7
LCCN 2002112732

Published by
North Country Publishing
355 Heidtman Road
Skandia, Michigan 49885
E-mail: northco@up.net
www.northcountrypublishing.com
Toll free:1-866-942-7898

Printed in the United States of America
Photographic Reproduction—Photomaster, Marquette, MI; Superior View Studio,
Marquette, MI; the State Archives of Michigan, Lansing, MI
Book and Cover Design—Holly Miller, Salt River Graphics, Shepherd, MI
10 9 8 7 6 5 4 3 2 1

For Lynn McGlothlin Emerick

ALSO BY LON EMERICK

The Superior Peninsula: Seasons in the Upper Peninsula of Michigan

*Sharing the Journey: Lessons from My Students
and Clients with Tangled Tongues*

That's Easy for You to Say: An Assault on Stuttering

With Stick and String: Adventures with Bow and Arrow

ONE

I t is a glorious day in late September and I am going on a pilgrimage to Central, a ghost town in the Keweenaw Peninsula of Northern Michigan. I shall go on a sojourn to the homesite of my forebears and seek their tidings across the years. More than a century-and-a-half ago, my Cornish ancestors toiled in the mine there and chiseled a livelihood and a heritage from the ancient copper-bearing rock. They also made a place for me in this remote and beautiful land.

Most of us who reside in the Upper Peninsula of Michigan are very aware of our heritage. Our roots are close at hand. Every day we see the landscape which our families saw, and their pioneer spirit pervades and enriches our lives. Will the legacy I leave in my turn continue to nurture and inspire the generations yet to come? Pondering this thought, I remember something Edmund Burke wrote long ago:

"People will not look forward to posterity
who never looked backward to their ancestors."

So, now in the autumn of my life, I set out on a sentimental journey to celebrate and honor the brave and enduring generations which came before me. It is time to look backward for the stepping stones my family left so that I may compass my own passage to the future.

Even though my goal is the former village of Central, I intend my quest to be an odyssey of discovery, not solely a destination. My mission is to learn more about the lives and times of my Celtic predecessors, yet along the way I will strive to listen for tales of the land and the unique and sturdy people who reside in this Superior Peninsula. But before I can begin my journey, I need to take my daily saunter on our beloved Foster Creek Homestead.

It is early fall and Jack Frost has been nipping at the maples—leaves in hues of lemon, scarlet and tangerine flutter in the cool breeze and decorate the woodland path. The air is light, luminous and the sky is exquisite cobalt. The pungent aroma of freshly-fallen leaves rises like a soothing balm at each footfall.

The forest is going about its annual metamorphosis and I, too, am transformed. The liturgy of autumn alters human minds and moods as well as leaves, ferns and migratory birds. The season of ripeness and harvest invigorates my spirit; yet there is a subtle flavor of melancholy, a lingering reverie of long summer days and care-free vacation memories.

I pause to rest on a steep ridge where my wife, Lynn, has erected a simple wooden sign in memory of my mother. As I sit amid the beautiful colors of this land my mother's bequest allowed us to purchase, I feel her reaching out in love to me one last time. So overcome am I by the ache of years long gone that I have to lean back against a maple tree and surrender to the memories which spill into my consciousness.

Born in Calumet near the turn of the twentieth century, Gertrude Mary Harris Emerick was a daughter of the Upper Peninsula. In her youth her heart was claimed by this beautiful peninsula and her passion for the Superior Lake, the flinty hills and dense forests never diminished. She felt—even as I now feel—blessed with the opportunity to dwell in a unique and wondrous land.

My mother's family came from Cornwall, a remote duchy of highly independent Celts in the far west of England. Cornwall is, in many respects, a lot like the Upper Peninsula of Michigan—an intriguing blend of rock, water and vast expanses of green. The Cornish are great bakers, sing like angels and are known worldwide as prodigious copper miners. When ore was discovered in the Keweenaw Peninsula, a rocky finger of granite which curves out into Lake Superior, the call went out for hardrock Cornish miners. In some cases, other workers refused to enter a mine unless led and supervised by a "Cousin Jack," a label given to miners from Cornwall who always seemed to have another cousin back in the old country when additional workers were needed.

My mother loved the life in Calumet. Despite the harsh climate and isolation, the city crackled with growth. The population in the area topped 100,000 and they had all the amenities, including a new opera house that featured well-known performers like John Philip Sousa, Lillian Russell and Sarah Bernhardt.

But it all came asunder in 1913 after a prolonged and bitter labor dispute. Economic times were hard then in the Upper Peninsula. In order to provide a better life for his family, my grandfather moved from Calumet to Detroit, where he worked for many decades for the Ford Motor Company. Gertrude married, raised four children, became a grandmother. She built a life in a suburb of Detroit. Days, months, years slipped by.

But she always felt like an exile in the cities far from her beloved North Country. The occasional visit to the Copper Country only served to magnify the gulf between her suburban lifestyle and the space and solitude of the land up north.

Although most of my colleagues advised against it, I knew my mother would understand when, spurning offers from prestigious universities in the Midwest, I chose a position at the much smaller Northern Michigan University. In the almost four decades since, I have never regretted taking the path less traveled. I am exactly where I was meant to be.

All the while my family was reveling in the Upper Peninsula good life, Mother was quietly assembling a small legacy to leave her sons. For many years she worked long hours at a Kresge's department store and put her wages into stock of the company which in future years became K-Mart. Its substantial growth must have been a poignant pleasure for someone who had endured the privations of the Great Depression. I was astonished and very touched when the check arrived following the settlement of her estate.

What could I do with the unexpected and generous bequest that would serve as a fitting tribute to this daughter of the U.P.? I didn't need more things; there were too many to keep track of already. It didn't take me more than a few minutes to find just the right answer: Land.

My mother and I shared a devotion to this harsh and beautiful place. So, we would obtain land near our home in West Branch Township, an idyllically pastoral area with huge farm fields, gorgeous upland forests and densely wooded river bottoms. The forty acres we were able to purchase with Mother's legacy has high wooded ridges, maple and conifer groves, a small open meadow with a carpet of wildflowers and, most of all, the rightness of this use of Mother's gift.

So, now I must go back to Old Central and see what lessons my maternal ancestors left for me among the crumbling ruins and piles of waste rock. No Cornish family would have survived the rigors of those early years without personal courage and persistence. There is much that I can learn from those proud and industrious pioneers. The Satterlys and Trezonas, the Trelawnys and Penhales, the Chewidden and Harris families were tenacious and resilient even in times of loss. Their life stories will offer a stable base for the trials of my own life.

A recurrence of cancer has given my excursion to Central a renewed sense of urgency. There is something about an encounter with mortality that enhances one's focus on the important things of life. Indeed, I have come to see the disease I have as a gift, a gift which helps me live better and more fully each day. The specter of death waiting just offstage stimulates me to greet each morning with anticipation and wonder and to focus on the joys of being alive. Rachel Carson, herself a cancer patient, advised us to try to look at things in our natural world as if it were the last time you might see them. An old Irish proverb says the same thing in a different way:

> *Dance as if no one were watching,*
> *Sing as if no one were listening,*
> *and live every day as if it were your last.*

And so it is on this September morn. I cannot afford to delay my generational pilgrimage to the Copper Country any longer.

Yet I linger, reluctant to leave the Homestead. Each of us, I believe, has a special landscape that resonates in our spirit; a major quest of life is to find such a place. Since we discovered this unique spot a few years ago, it has buried itself deep inside my heart and I feel a strange unease when I am anywhere else. I know every centimeter of our eighty-acre haven. I know where three old growth sugar maple trees—survivors of the logging blitzkrieg many years ago—reach for the sky. I know where a red-tailed hawk has its nest in a gnarled yellow birch. If I linger by the edge of Foster Creek, I may see a whitetail deer browsing on red osier or catch a glimpse of a shy pine marten chasing a red squirrel. Although the resident barred owls are napping now, this evening I would hear them gossiping in the conifer grove they call home.

I rejoice in my personal connection to this land; every day I give thanks that I am privileged to live here. Many persons seem to view their natural surroundings as a backdrop for their lives; they would be doing the same things whether they lived in Marquette, Missoula or Monterey. But if you seek a place where your spirit will flourish—and I do not believe one's spirit can flourish without a personal relationship to the earth—the place in turn will soothe, inspire and shape your life in a myriad of positive ways.

So I tarry in the exotically-colored forest, worried that I may miss some woodland drama in my absence. Will a migrating Swainson's thrush or white-throated sparrow pass through without my greetings? Will I miss some ephemeral seasonal fragrance or a particularly delicate play of light in my favorite maple copse?

Perhaps I will be ready to leave if I saunter once more back to a small clearing in the forest where I have erected Woodhenge, a pine replica of Stonehenge, in tribute to my Celtic ancestors. I pass all the familiar natural features as I follow an old tote road. Pausing along the way, I greet the discarded vehicles enjoying eternal repose beside the road. When I first saw these rusty relics shortly after acquiring the land, I was annoyed, and explored the idea of hiring a junk dealer to haul the eyesores away. But upon reflection, I shifted my paradigm: These old cars are historical artifacts. Right there, leaning precariously on its side against a pine stump, is the '36 Chevrolet coupe which belonged to Uncle Louie. The manufacturer's metal seal, still readable, is riveted inside the engine compartment. It says:

Chevrolet Division
General Motors Corporation
Style No 36-1017

Body No F 2622
Trim No 3
Paint No 206
Body by Fisher

When Louie came home from the horror that was Guadalcanal, he was unable to cope with the complexities of civilian life. He built a small, solitary cabin, helped out on his father's farm, did some work in the woods in the winter. A little further along the trail, resting on its roof, is the 1939 Dodge panel truck which family patriarch, Karl Bjork, used to haul eggs and produce into town to sell at local stores. It still has several oak floor boards—in fairly good shape—from the era when wood was used in the manufacturing of cars. Finally, a vintage Ford "Woody," one of the first station wagons made in Detroit, sits in the deep shade under a large hemlock tree.

As I saunter along the final turn in the road, there, sitting erect and attentive on the lintel over the portal to Woodhenge, is a mature broad-winged hawk. The bird scans me with imperious disdain and then slowly lifts and sails silently into the woods.

What an exhilarating event—a wild creature accepting my creation, even blessing it by his presence. Taking the archdruid's seat in the circle of wooden trilithons, I reflect on this special occurrence. Native Americans consider hawks and eagles—masters of the sky called raptors—to be birds of power and guardian spirits of the natural world. Birds figured largely in Celtic mythology also, because they dwell in an intermediary realm between earth and the spirit world.

Finally now, I am ready to make my pilgrimage to Central. As I rise to leave, I touch the old logs of Woodhenge salvaged from a supply a prior owner intended to use to build a cabin. Slowly, reverently, I retrace my steps back through the brightly colored forest to our log home.

Our house is situated well back from a township macadam road on the very edge of a heavily forested ravine. Tall maples and a pair of large hemlocks press close, providing dense shade and a haven for birds and other forest creatures. Finches, nuthatches and chickadees flit close by and provide a daily symphony of natural music. We have deer, porcupines and raccoons for our nearest neighbors; during one unseasonably mild December we watched a weasel clad in its stark white ermine raiment scampering over bare brown ground. Just this fall, after several years of looking, we observed a mature bobcat hunting rodents under the birdfeeders. One hot day last summer, a large black bear wandered through our yard, stood up, placed his muddy paws on the lower level windows and peered inside.

Foster Creek Homestead

Lon Emerick

Woodhenge

Lon Emerick

Autumn transformation

A small, intermittent stream courses down through the ravine. I have named it Lynn's *Shruhan*, a Gaelic word meaning brook, in honor of my wife's Scottish heritage. This wee brook flows into a tiny pond and then into a branch of Foster Creek, a somewhat larger stream that defines the western border of the Homestead. In spring, we are entertained by a chorus of frogs, a sure sign that the long white winter season is over. Since we dwell within the woods, the outdoors becomes a part of our living space.

The Foster Creek Homestead is located in Section 11 of West Branch Township in southeastern Marquette County; the township, T46N, R24W, includes 56 square miles which form a perfect square, and hence the motto, "The Perfect Township."

West Branch Township celebrated its 100th anniversary in 1995, the year we moved into our home. Many of the descendants of the original Scandinavian and German pioneers still live here; their names, Heidtman, Boyer, Beckman, Shaw and Johnson are also given to local roads. When I walk or cycle about the area, I am awed by the heroic efforts it must have taken to clear the land for farming.

The Township is located right on the dividing line between the two distinct land formations of the Upper Peninsula. To the west and north are the Superior Highlands, worn-down remnants of huge mountains, the Laurentian or Canadian Shield. Here you find a mixture of igneous and metamorphic rock types, such as gneiss, basalt and granite. The land is flinty with granite knobs and looks as if the bare bones of the planet are jutting out. It is hardly a land for cultivation.

So the immigrant farmers looked east to the second and more promising land formation, sedimentary lake plains deposited eons ago by ancient seas. Technically termed Northern Lacustrine, the land is low relief and contains glacial deposits of clay and sand. The bedrock in this region is sandstone and limestone.

I take one last loving look around our yard as I carry my notebooks, camera and tape recorder to my truck, which is waiting eagerly by the garage. The Silver Shrike is the most recent of a series of compact Chevrolet pickups I have owned. All were named for birds.

As was the case with his predecessors, the Shrike has a distinct personality. Like the striking gray raptor, the northern shrike, for which he is named, the current truck is mercurial, impatient and yearns to be on the move.

It is expected that men have some interest in and an aptitude for the mechanical aspects of vehicles. I have neither. When Bob, the salesman at the Chevrolet dealer, opened the Silver Shrike's hood to show me the engine—an obligatory male ritual—I recognized nothing, not a single item, in the crammed compartment. But I treat my trucks as living beings and lavish lots of personal attention on them. They are kept well-serviced with all the appropriate body fluids and are always shiningly immaculate. The Silver Shrike also carries distinctive license plates and he seems to revel in his uniqueness, especially when parked in a crowded lot with many other vehicles.

On the rear bumper is an official State of Michigan license plate; however, it is personalized and proclaims, *Kernow* 3. The word *Kernow* means Cornwall in the ancient language of that land. The number three is included because Celtic peoples regarded that number as mysterious and powerful.

The front plate is all Cornish. It features the flag of St. Piran (sometimes spelled Perran or Pirin), the patron saint of Cornwall: A white cross on a field of black. Piran came to the coast of Cornwall from Ireland (or perhaps Wales) in the Fifth century to spread the message of Christianity to the Celts.

Landing on the coast in a fragile boat made of animal hides, he founded his mission with the tin miners. These early Cornish workers mined tin by building fires on ore-bearing rock and then catching the molten metal as it dripped down the cracks and channels. The metal was traded to Phoenicians and other Mediterranean seafarers who sought the tin to blend with copper for making bronze weapons and other implements.

Showing his solidarity with the miners' difficult lives, St. Piran fashioned his personal banner to reflect their labors: The black field represented the dark ore-bearing rock and the white cross symbolized the tin which melted down from the boulders.

In addition to the national flag of Cornwall, the license plate features the triangular shield of the Cornish hero, Cadoc, who lost his life resisting the Norman invasion of the British Isles. The shield is black and on the front is a triangular pattern of golden bosses or roundels:

Directly under the shield is written the motto of Cornwall, "One and all" in both English and Cornish, *onen hagoll*. There is little doubt that the Silver Shrike carries a son of Cornwall in its cab.

At long last, the Silver Shrike and I wheel out our driveway and head down Heidtman Road to the east. We reach the highway and then turn north. This is the same U.S. 41 Highway that extends from Copper Harbor at the very tip of the Keweenaw Peninsula all the way to Miami, Florida, a total of 1,990 miles.

My pretty Muse sits on the dashboard and her shy smile tells me that she is happy to be going on this pilgrimage. When I retired from the university to start a new life as a literary naturalist, my diminutive Muse appeared to encourage my efforts. Only eighteen inches tall, she has long auburn hair, dark, limpid eyes, and a delicate oval face with high cheek bones. In her long, pale green diaphanous gown, she is almost the mirror image of Jane Seymour. My Muse does not speak nor does she ever look directly at me. But when my work is going well, when the phrases are flowing off my pen, she hums a tune, faintly, that reminds me of Greensleeves and swings her tiny legs in time to the click of my old portable typewriter.

Whenever I talk about my former lifetime as a professor of speech pathology, or even glance at one of the textbooks I wrote during that period, my Muse flees. I think she may be frightened of the overseer that drove me relentlessly during the tedious process of penning those scholarly works. Otto was his name. A butcher by trade, he scrutinized my progress with somber malevolence. His immense bulk was garbed in a white apron, well-spattered with blood and other unspeakable gore. As I labored over footnotes and indexes, Otto paced around my study continually tapping the blunt end of a meat cleaver into his enormous palm. Thankfully, Otto has been gone for more than a decade now and I grin broadly as my wee Muse, the Silver Shrike and I approach Green Garden Hill.

TWO

The Silver Shrike purrs happily as we follow the highway between large farm fields on Green Garden Hill. On this bluebird autumn morning, it is difficult to imagine the ferocity of winter storms which sometimes sweep this open area, bringing swirling snow and creating immense drifts. One Thanksgiving weekend, *Heikki Lunta*, the Finnish snow sprite, made a memorable visit to Green Garden Hill.

An oral tradition in the Upper Peninsula maintains that each winter will have two major storms, one at Thanksgiving and the other on St. Patrick's Day. There are even some longtime residents—our former neighbor of thirty years among them—who view inclement weather as punishment for warm summers and mild autumns. So, when snow storms do occur on these dates, they nod and mutter with grim satisfaction: "I told you we were going to pay for all them nice days."

Consequently, it was no surprise to many Old Timers when a swirling blizzard struck Marquette County on November 27, 1966, the Sunday after Thanksgiving. It started with freezing rain and then blinding snow, blown by winds of twenty to thirty miles per hour, with gusts up to sixty miles per hour. Drifts piled up on the roads and road crews could not keep up with the intensity of the storm. In some places on Green Garden Hill, drifts of eight and nine feet trapped hundreds of university students and other travelers returning from Thanksgiving vacation. The stranded travelers abandoned their vehicles and sought shelter wherever they could. Many were taken in by gracious residents along the highway, but most headed for the Idle Time Bar.

Imagine, if you will, more than 350 young people, mostly students from Northern Michigan University and Michigan Technological University, hunkered down in a rural tavern. The Idle Time Bar had no power, no heat, a limited amount of food, and only a single kerosene lamp for illumination. The supply of liquid refreshments, of course, did not survive for long. Sometime during the night, the toilets plugged up. The stranded travelers talked, drank spirits and dozed on the floor. Heather Shaefer, a junior at Northern Michigan University, reported that the students got along fairly well in the cold, cramped redoubt but by the time the highways were finally cleared at 3:00 p.m. on Monday, many people were noticeably cranky.

The road crews worked through the long, blustery night to open U.S. 41. But each time they made a swath through the immense snowbanks, the road drifted shut behind them. Even huge snow removal equipment became mired in the heavy, wet snow. On Monday, after the wind and snow abated, crews set to work with large rotary snow plows. Many drivers had abandoned their vehicles on or close to the roadway. One snow removal worker is said to have chewed up a Volkswagen Beetle with his rotary plow. When he observed red pieces of metal spewing out of the blower spout he stopped his machine, but by then the small car was almost chewed to shreds. Many years later I asked a retired road worker if the story was true. After a long pause, he looked at me with a small smile and said enigmatically, "Could be."

When I gaze at the huge farm fields of Green Garden Hill, I am always awed by the enormous energy it must have taken these early settlers to clear the land, plant the crops and build their sturdy barns. The new residents still found time to build a school and then a church. Fortunately, I happened to meet Mrs. Mabel Koepp LeMaire, granddaughter of one of the four German immigrants who founded Green Garden, the first agricultural community in the Upper Peninsula. Mabel, a delightfully engaging octogenarian, still resides in her ancestral homestead and is the unofficial historian-laureate of the community. She knows the area well.

In 1862, four German immigrant farmers got off the boat at Marquette Harbor. Looking around, they were dismayed by the dense pine forests, granite outcroppings and piles of iron ore on the docks. Noticing their dismay, a seaman advised them to head southeast to what was then called Kawbawgam Hill. Charles Kawbawgam, one of the last Ojibwa leaders in the region, had a residence by a spring on the crest of the hill. Here, Ludwig Koepp, Carl Kunde, Siegfried Zerbel and Julius Zerbel found the demarcation line between the granite highlands and the low relief alluvial plains. The industrious and devout farmers sank their future into the soil. Religious services were held first in the farmers' homes and then in the school house. In 1889, the men of the community banded together to erect a red brick *Kirche*; the descendants are proud that their frugal German forebears built St. Paul's Evangelical Lutheran Church for only $1,700. Later, stained glass windows crafted in Germany were added.

"My grandfather, Ludwig (Louis) Koepp, donated the land for the church," said Mrs. LeMaire as she proudly gave me a tour of the sturdy building. "'Here's a pamphlet we printed in 1988, and it tells all about the history of St. Paul's," she added as we emerged into the autumn sunlight. Glancing down through the list of pastors who have served the congregation, I noticed the name Reverend C. S. Hollerup. Without thinking, I read his name aloud and, unable to control my amusement, related the time I inadvertently saw a Methodist preacher's marginal notes on a typed copy of his sermon. Midway down the second page, on the right-hand margin, he had scribbled this instruction to himself: "Talk loudly, evidence here weak." I could tell that Mabel was not amused by my anecdote so I shifted gears and asked why the immigrant community was called Green Garden.

"My father, Willard Koepp," she said, "named his homestead 'Elysia Farm' because it seemed like a paradise to him. Then one summer day as a group of farmers strolled after church and stopped to admire the farms spread out on the hill, someone said, 'It looks like a beautiful green garden.'" Green Garden was quite a thriving community. The residents had a school, the solid brick church, a general store, a candy store run by Mrs. Basal and even their own post office. Mrs. LeMaire told me that after Chief Kawbawgam's death the community acquired his home to use as a Grange Hall.

"We had lots of dances in the Hall," she said with a smile, remembering the old days. "It was not a very large building and when all of us got moving to the music, the floor would roll and pitch!"

U.S. Highway 41 stretches ahead, newly resurfaced and with nary a roll or pitch. First paved in 1927, this roadway—originally called the Marquette to Bay de Noc State Road—was a dusty path in the summer and deep muddy ruts at other seasons. Now, as I approach the crest of Green Garden Hill, my anticipation quickens, for I am almost upon one of my favorite Upper Peninsula vistas. There, spread out before me in full autumn color panorama, are the hills surrounding the city of Marquette. Remnants of an ancient mountain range, they extend far to the north. Covered by a vast forest of maple and birch, the brightly colored leaves contrast with the wide crown and deep green of the Upper Peninsula's signature tree, the eastern white pine. Lake Superior, the immense 'blue profound,' spreads out to the distant horizon.

The hills are alive with fond memories. Before finding our beloved Foster Creek Homestead, we lived for almost thirty years in Shiras Hills, a cluster of houses in south Marquette nestled in close proximity to the granite remnants. We know these hills, and the Carp River Valley which slices through them, like old friends. In fact, we have named several distinctive features in the area after particularly memorable visits. A high crag from which we can watch the nuances of Lake Superior is Lynn's Lookout; a long bench of granite where we spent a delightful winter afternoon baking bread strips rolled on green sticks is Sourdough Ridge; Summit Peak, with its expanse of rose-colored gneiss which we scaled one wet spring day, is the highest point in the area.

Several summers ago, Northern Michigan University hosted an all-class reunion for alumni and I managed to visit with several former students. One young woman, now in her forties, reminded me of a six-mile snowshoe trek a group of students and I had taken in the granite hills more than two decades ago. A troop of eager undergraduates and the professor scaled Migisy Bluff, inched carefully across frozen Lake Buschell and wound our way through the snowy forest. After crossing the Carp River precariously on a slippery log, we tumbled into my home and celebrated our adventure with a pizza party. As Nancy reminisced about our trek of so long ago, her eyes sparkled.

"You know," she said finally, "I've forgotten most of the classroom lectures, but that snowshoe hike is still vivid in my mind." Same here.

Caught up in reverie, I find myself driving through Harvey, a village named after a sales representative of the Fairbanks Scale Company. Have you heard the one about the traveling salesman from Connecticut and the clergyman's daughter? Well, Charles Thompson Harvey stayed at the Baptist Mission boardinghouse in Sault Saint Marie while recuperating from typhoid fever. There he was befriended by Reverend Bingham's daughter, Kate.

The lovely Kate was delighted to show Harvey the bustling frontier town. An active, restless young man of twenty-two years, Harvey was fascinated with the laborious unloading, portaging and reloading of the many sailing vessels which could not traverse the falls and rapids of the St. Mary's River connecting Lake Huron with Lake Superior. Although experienced in neither engineering nor heavy construction, Harvey turned his youthful enthusiasm into the idea of constructing a water lock to lower and raise ships between Lake Superior and the less turbulent waters of the lower St. Mary's River.

They laughed when Charles Harvey sat down to plan a canal. Indeed, some locals—particularly those with a vested interest in the portaging enterprise—were actively hostile toward the young salesman. Both Daniel Webster and Henry Clay condemned the project in the U.S. Senate as a flagrant waste of money in a worthless wilderness; yet on August 26, 1852, President Millard Fillmore signed a bill awarding a substantial grant to Harvey.

On June 7, 1853, the young salesman pushed the first wheelbarrow of dirt out of the cut. Despite the frigid cold, an epidemic of cholera and dysentery, inadequate machinery—Harvey invented a steam hammer on the spot—and the difficulty of cutting through Cambrian rock, 1,600 men completed the project on schedule. The first lock was 350 feet long and 70 feet wide. The canal opened on June 18, 1855. The first ship to go through the locks was the northbound *Illinois*, a side-wheel steamer under the guidance of Captain Jack Wilson.

Young Harvey did not long rest on his lock-building laurels. After marrying Miss Kate Bingham, he headed west along the south shore of Lake Superior until he came to the burgeoning new city of Marquette. Like so many others before him, and since, he fell in love with the area. On land he had been awarded by the Federal government for his success at the Soo, he laid out a village in his name and then turned his immense energy to other enterprises. First, he built a blast furnace at the mouth of the Chocolay River (French explorers named the river "chocolate" because of the dark brown color of the water), erected a sawmill and explored the prospect of building roads and railways. He also constructed a large home which he dubbed "Bayou House" on a loop of the Chocolay River.

The Harvey Home still stands beside the Chocolay River. After Bayou House burned to the ground in 1865, Harvey rebuilt it even more lavishly. When he was away attending to his many enterprises, his spinster sisters lived in the two-story colonial home. Local residents called it the "Old Maids' House." The house has gone through several reincarnations over the years—a private residence, a bed and breakfast inn and now a veterinary clinic.

Charles T. Harvey eventually sought his fortune in New York City. In the Big Apple, then a much smaller McIntosh, Harvey designed and built the very first elevated rail system, the EL, in 1874. His life then took a downward spiral, and the man who conceived and built the now famous locks at Sault Ste. Marie died penniless and alone in a seedy hotel in New York within view of the EL on March 14, 1912. I wonder if in those last difficult years Harvey yearned for the Lake Superior country of his youth.

The highway curves gently toward the west and there, on my right, is the reason why so many of us could never live happily anywhere else: The Superior Lake. I pull into the Department of Transportation Welcome Center, a large log house filled with information about the Peninsula, and walk out on the bike path toward the city of Marquette. Today the Lake is a deep indigo and shimmers in the slanting morning sunlight. Suddenly, my passion for this greatest of the Great Lakes overwhelms me as it always does, and I need to find a vantage point affording a better, a longer view. I must climb atop the Rock Cut and make a personal offering to Gitche Gumee.

Crossing the busy highway, I thread my way through the detritus left behind when a local hardware store closed its doors the previous summer. The rocky path takes me uphill through a grove of pines and then onto a flat expanse of ancient rock, schists and quartzite remnants of mountains that, nearly two billion years ago, were as high as the Alps. Early settlers called this high granite shelf First Point and quarried rock here in the early twentieth century. Evidence of their labors— long vertical grooves—can still be seen.

But the real attraction from this rocky point is the vista of Lake Superior. The view is stunning even for a longtime lover of the Lake. Paraphrasing Captain William Clark's excited cry when the Corps of Discovery reached the Pacific Ocean, I say aloud, "Lake Superior in view! Oh, the joy!" Taking a precarious seat on the edge of the precipice, I am exhilarated by the immensity of the ice water mansions; the lake stretches out to the horizon, all the way to Canada, almost 160 miles north. Let me confess it: Here is my ecological address; the aura from this gorgeous body of water has seeped into my DNA. Even geologists J. W. Foster and J. D. Whitney were sufficiently impressed to include this passage in their otherwise sober report in 1850:

> *Lake Superior possesses all the sublimity of the ocean. In gazing upon its surface, whether stretched out like a vast mirror, reflecting the varying tints of the sky, or ruffled by gently-curling waves, or lashed by the fury of the storm, the beholder is alike impressed with a feeling of the grand and the infinite.*

No question about it, Lake Superior is a dominant force in this region. It is like a good and constant companion—cold, aloof and capricious, to be sure—and a source of inspiration. We feel the lake's influence on our thoughts, our moods, our entire lives; its presence is commanding. Lake Superior even influences the weather in the area. Near the shoreline, winter temperatures may be as much as twenty degrees warmer than in the interior; in summer the situation is reversed and the lake acts as a giant air conditioner. It is no wonder that the Indians called it *Gitche Gumee*, the Great-Sea-Shining-Water, and worshiped the lake as a deity. It is difficult to talk about this clear inland sea except in superlatives.

Consider its vital statistics:

- greatest width from east to west 350 miles

- greatest width from north to south 160 miles

- greatest depth 1,555 feet; average depth 472 feet

- covers 51,700 square miles. It could hold Rhode Island, Connecticut and three states the size of Massachusetts inside its borders

- has 2,796 miles of shoreline

The dimensions are reason enough for the name "Superior," although according to historians the appellation was a fortuitous occurrence. When early French explorers first discovered the huge body of water lying north of Lake Huron, they referred to it as *le lac Superieur*, or "the upper lake," and so labeled it on their maps. At one time the lake was dedicated as Lac Tracy in honor of a French government official. However, the nickname "Superior" persisted and now no other name seems appropriate.

All the superlatives about Lake Superior are true. It is the largest, coldest (maintaining an overall temperature of about forty-two degrees Fahrenheit year round), deepest and roughest of the Great Lakes. It is also the cleanest. As I admire the Lake shimmering in the autumn sun, it is hard to believe this robust body of water is terribly fragile.

Yet, despite its immense proportions, its awesome power and pristine clarity, Lake Superior *is* a fragile and vulnerable jewel. Fragile because it is still young in a biological sense and its waters drain very slowly; experts estimate it would take at least five hundred years for Lake Superior to purge itself of impurities. (By comparison, Lake Erie can cleanse itself in twenty years.) Vulnerable because of the outrageous bureaucratic notion that, since the lake is so clean, we can permit pollution up to a certain level, one established by monitoring an already dirty body of water in another area. Fragile and vulnerable because—and this is the heart of it—the idea prevails that our natural resources are inexhaustible.

For all who love Lake Superior, the pivotal question is this: Is *any* economic gain worth the price we pay in the decline of water quality? Can we endorse *any* development which results in the warning that children and women of childbearing age should not consume fish taken from what was once the purest lake? Can we agree to *any* action, such as siphoning off water for sale to parched regions, which may have dire consequences for the ecological balance of the Peninsula's entire watershed?

I ponder these issues as I listen to the music of the waves upon the shore and savor the fresh smell of the breeze blowing over miles of open water. What would the Ojibwa say? What would the early French explorers, Radisson, Chouart and Groseilliers think about the current dilemma?

I am reluctant to leave the rocky promontory but I have ancestral promises to keep and miles to go before I reach Central. Besides, I shall see the Superior Lake again sixty miles up the road. Leaving a small offering of sage under a young pine tree, I pick my way down the ridge to the Silver Shrike.

The Silver Shrike is sulky and refuses to turn over on the first crank. Typical male, he is impatient to be on the road, eating up the miles, making time. My Muse is bemused by it all and wears her Mona Lisa smile. When I proceed less than a mile and turn into Marquette Prison, the truck coughs in disgust.

Lon Emerick

Mabel LeMaire, historian laureate of Green Garden

Lon Emerick

Lake Superior, the Blue Profound

Lon Emerick

Marquette Branch Prison gardens

Driving slowly, I make a loop by the administration building, a striking old structure. Built in 1899 of regional sandstone, the building resembles a Norman castle complete with towers and turrets. All it lacks is a moat. But, softening the dark, formidable structure is an expansive flower garden complete with a large stone frog squirting a stream of water into a pond. Behind the administration building are the grim structures and high walls where the inmates, all of them judged to be very bad dudes, are doing hard time.

When you first meet Mathew Obiden you would never guess that he labored for thirty-one years inside the walls of a maximum security prison as a correctional officer. With his friendly, open manner and dark good looks, Matt seems more like a pastor of a small town church or a popular high school civics teacher. But then you notice his eyes: they crackle with intensity and miss nothing, not even the slightest movement.

"I remember vividly the first time I entered those walls," Matt said one day over coffee. "It was 1970. I looked around at all the big, tough-looking guys, guards and inmates, and thought, 'Here I am only five feet, six inches.' And, at that time, new guards had little formal training."

"How do you keep your sanity on a job like that?" I asked.

Matt paused for a long moment and then replied, "It's tough. When those barred gates clanked shut behind me that first week, I almost had a panic attack. If I needed to get out of there in a hurry, would they let me out? There's a lot of stress being a correctional officer. But I have a good family life . . . and a sense of humor helps, too."

"Working with all those cons, don't officers become paranoid after awhile?"

"Well, sure. I remember automatically checking the grocery bags my wife brought home from the market to see if there was any contraband."

"Quite an occupational hazard, huh?"

"You learn quick in this business. You learn to read the inmates. The hostile ones are easy—you always have to be wary of them. A few try to be your friend, to ingratiate themselves with you. But it's the noncommittal, quiet ones that scare most of us. You never know what they might do."

While working full-time, Matt earned a university degree in corrections. He retired not long ago as a captain.

"Any success stories?" I queried.

"Not many," Matt responded, "The men in there are tough, really bad characters, the worst of the worst."

The waitress came by and filled our coffee cups.

"There *was* one man," continued Matt, "I saw him in a hotel downstate. Traverse City, I think. I was bringing our bags into a room when this guy—he looked kind of familiar—stopped sweeping the floor and came over. He reached out and shook my hand. 'You may not remember me, Cap, I'm Charles Denman. I got this here job and I ain't ever going back to the joint.' He turned to leave and then came back. 'Thanks for being straight with me, Cap; you never promised nothing you couldn't deliver. That meant a lot.'"

A small victory to be sure, but small victories enable men and women like Matt Obiden to continue day after day. As I pull out of the prison grounds, I decide to stop at the gift shop and buy a postcard depicting the striking old administration building. I will send the card to my friend Bill, with the cryptic message, "Wish you were here." Usually I send him memorabilia featuring cows, a standing joke between us for the past decade. As a retired dairy farmer, Bill never wants to see another cow and is bemused by the constant stream of Holstein items I send him. He and his wife Joan, far from acting annoyed by towels, plush toys, hats and notepaper depicting black and white cows, look forward to the next package. Bill will get a kick out of the postcard and will know instantly who sent it.

Instead of going through Marquette, I will take the so-called bypass around the south edge of the city. This lovely town of 21,000 on the south shore of Lake Superior was founded by a small group of visionary men who saw the prospect of a port city for shipping iron ore from the newly discovered mines located ten miles to the west. Initially, the new port was named Worchester in honor of the Massachusetts hometown of Amos Harlow, an entrepreneur who secured the equipment to build the first ore dock.

Thankfully, after flirting with the name Carp River, the city fathers decided to honor Father Jacques Marquette, a Jesuit missionary who explored the south shore of Lake Superior to harvest souls in the seventeenth century. Legend has it that Marquette said mass at or near the present day Lighthouse Point in June of 1671. The city of Marquette was incorporated almost exactly two hundred years later.

As I proceed along the bypass, I look up as I always do at a large granite knob. Burt's Peak, also called the Giant's Foot, offers a commanding view of the south Marquette Harbor. A hundred years ago a splendid resort, called the Hotel Superior, stood on that hill and it was there that my maternal grandparents came for their honeymoon in June 1901.

The hotel was gorgeous, complete with gothic towers and a five hundred-foot veranda. Built lavishly of native white pine in 1891, it was five stories high and had 241 rooms. It even featured its own band. Located on twenty-seven well-landscaped acres, some of the food prepared for the guests was supplied by the hotel farm. In the young town of Marquette, the Superior Hotel was the place to stay.

Superior Hotel, Marquette, Michigan, 1901

I am afraid all the opulence of the Superior Hotel was lost on the newlywed Alfred Harris and Gertrude Satterly. The Sixty-Seven Year Cornish War had already started in the back of the Methodist church in Calumet, right after the wedding ceremony.

One of the guests, a young woman named Rachel Pendarvis, recently immigrated from my grandfather's hometown of St. Austell, Cornwall, approached the bride and groom in the receiving line and lamented loudly, "Oh, Alfie, what about poor Sadie you left behind in the Old Country?" That was the remark that launched a thousand skirmishes in that marriage.

It must have been a tense journey on the afternoon train from Calumet to Marquette. That night, as the young couple finally settled into their hotel room, tired and tense, Grandfather took off his trousers, turned to his tiny new bride and commanded, "Here, put these on." She looked at him in astonishment and replied, "Al, you know I can't wear your pants." Grandfather nodded emphatically and said, "That's right, Woman, and don't ever forget that." In all the years I knew them he never called Gertrude anything other than "Woman."

They were two very different people, more so than any married couple I have ever known. Grandfather was tough, taciturn and determinedly independent. Although at five feet, ten inches tall he was not a large man, he carried himself with an easy confidence that other men noted. But it was his eyes that warned others: they blazed, "Don't tread on me!" His steely-blue, direct and unwavering gaze alerted more than one younger and larger man to back down from a confrontation.

And the "Old Man" had an awesome temper. Never one to suffer fools or idlers gladly, his responses were direct, peremptory and often blasphemous. "Goddamn it," he would explode in response to infractions or delays . . . "You bloody idiot!" But Grandfather liked me, perhaps because I was the only grandson who followed him about on his chores, explored his woods and was eager to be his hunting partner. Best of all, according to Grandfather, I didn't whine or chatter. Actually, I didn't talk much at all because I stuttered so badly. I was comforted by the same long silences he enjoyed and I was relieved that he never asked me the silly questions so many adults ask children.

When Grandfather did speak, he exhibited a characteristic Cornish dialect. All "h" sounds were omitted and (this really intrigued me) the "h" was added before most words beginning with a vowel. One day after sitting quietly by the back door of his rustic log cabin, the Old Man observed, "Lad, look at all those bloody hants going hup and down that 'emlock tree!" He also had several colorful sayings which, now that I am the Grandfather, I find myself repeating. After a period of rest following dinner, Grandfather would stand up and announce, "Well, Lad, I guess I'd better do something, even if it's wrong." I liked it when he said that. And when, as we reached the end of some chore—stacking cordwood or piling bales of hay—he would invariably say as he hefted the last piece, "'Ere's the one we've been looking for." I always wondered why we didn't find that bale first.

Much later in life, I learned why Grandfather was so physically and mentally tough. He learned the lessons early. The last of nine children born to a poverty-stricken family in Cornwall, Alfred was told by his father, Tom Harris, that he must leave the family and seek work in America. He was just sixteen years old when he boarded a ship and sailed to Boston, then sat up for three nights on a train making its way to the Upper Peninsula. The day after he arrived, my grandfather was working deep in a copper mine. The boy became a man very quickly; he never looked back or contacted his parents or siblings in the Old Country. Grandfather tolerated no weakness in himself . . . or others.

What a contrast to happy, bubbly Gertrude. Even if you scripted a latter-day sitcom, you could not come up with a married couple so different. Her parents could see this discordance and begged their daughter to delay getting married at sixteen while they helped her pursue her interests in music and art. But she would not listen to their doubts about her Cornish suitor.

Grandmother was a warm, sunny, wee lass, only four feet, ten inches, aggressively friendly, funny and full of mischief. She loved to talk. And she was almost pathologically energetic. When I stayed at their hardscrabble farm during summer vacations, Grandmother turned even household drudgery into an amusing contest. "See now," she would say in full flight, "You time me. I bet I'll be done by 9 a.m." Careening around the small cabin, she swept, washed, dusted and even had a strawberry-rhubarb pie in the oven of her wood-burning cookstove before the clock chimed nine times.

Grandmother, as a woman of unadulterated Cornish heritage, was a good cook and a world class baker. I think her skill with flour, shortening and spices comes in the Cornish genes. For sixty years she tried to get Grandfather to express approval of her efforts in the kitchen, but he always sat chewing silently. Many times she would ask, "Do you like the pie, Al?" And his response was always the same: "Well, I'm eating it, ain't I, Woman?"

She enjoyed feeding company and making visitors comfortable, almost to a fault. If you finished a plate of stew or some other dish, she would plop more down on your plate even before she asked if you wanted a second helping. One time when I was attending college, I came to visit my grandparents during the Thanksgiving holiday. The very minute I arrived, Grandmother insisted I have a piece of freshly-baked pumpkin pie. A nutritionally deprived student, weary of dorm food, I inhaled the pie in six bites. Grandmother laughed joyously. "Here, have another," she demanded. In less than fifteen minutes I had consumed the entire pie and she was ecstatic. The Old Man snorted in disgust and went out to feed the pig.

So the Cornish War went on for more than six decades.

Actually, I think my grandparents rather enjoyed the skirmishes; at least the battles and arguments appeared to be a *modus operandi* they saw as a means of sustaining their relationship. Divorce was out of the question. Once, after sixty years of marriage—sixty years!—they separated for almost a year. They were miserable apart. Not long before Grandmother died at eighty-three, I again was visiting. She proudly showed me the new twin beds they had purchased to replace the marital double bed they had shared for more than half a century.

"Grandmother!" I said with some surprise, looking at the beds on each side of the room, "Single beds after all these years?"

She looked at me with a devilish twinkle in her eyes and replied, "The walk will do the Old Fart good."

I laugh aloud remembering Grandmother's earthy riposte. The Silver Shrike is having a good time, too, on the four-lane bypass; his six-cylinder Vortec engine accelerates smartly to the 55 mile-per-hour speed limit. Little does the Shrike know that this silly bit of freeway is only two miles in length and soon we will have to resume city driving speeds. Soon, too, my amusement will segue to tension and irritation, for we are about to enter the most dangerous and visually appalling segment of the entire sojourn: the business corridor west of Marquette.

THREE

I am not looking forward to this passage from Marquette to the Iron Range. Here, U.S. 41 becomes a crowded commercial corridor all the way past Ishpeming. Therein lies the dilemma: how to negotiate the drive that tries my soul. The first part in particular, extending for about five miles—it seems much longer—is an ugly linear monument to consumerism and congestion. I must admit that I have helped to create this unsightly business district, this garish display of our contemporary heritage now found at the outskirts of every town of any size, by fulfilling my national obligation as a consumer.

Although I try my best, it is difficult to ignore what Kent Nerburn in his book, *Road Angels*, calls the Great American Drive-Through. The reality crowds in: two large shopping malls, every species of "mart," a giant hardware store, two furniture stores, several motels, five automobile dealerships, all the fast food bistros known to Western Civilization and last, but by no means least, the ubiquitous "convenience store," which offers gasoline (pump your own), tobacco products and high-calorie snacks.

Why didn't the developers and township planners work with the native vegetation and natural contours of the land? It seems that when the decision is made to build a huge warehouse store, the very first task is to conduct a campaign of scorched earth: cut all the trees, strip off the topsoil and bulldoze all the hills to create a flat plateau. Then, after erecting a large architecturally-challenged box, lay down a mammoth parking lot—in front of the store, facing the highway, of course.

And here's the thing: it didn't have to be this way. It seems like yesterday that I first came to Marquette to interview for a position on the faculty at Northern Michigan University. The decision to accept the offer at Northern was almost made by the time I drove the five hundred miles from Minnesota to Marquette. Weary from hours on the road, synapses eroded by traffic, I came over the crest of a hill just east of the airport and saw Lake Superior, framed between rock cuts on either side of the highway, stretching out to the horizon. The entrance to my soon-to-be adopted city was an esthetic delight.

We had a chance to be different here in this Superior Peninsula. Before we realized it, we morphed into a Generic City and many of the original features that made this someplace special have been replaced by trademark highway structures. Will we destroy the very reasons why we wished to live here? Native Americans lived by a truism which is still apt: "If you would build a house in the mountains, don't tear down the mountains."

But, say many local residents in a resigned tone of voice, growth is natural, indeed inevitable. "Progress, you can't stop it." Once, in a moment of weakness, I asked a township official, "Progress for what? How did the concept of *progress* become linked with time and quantity—why do we have to keep doing things faster, larger?" He looked at me as if I were intellectually-challenged and responded, "If you don't grow, you die . . . if the economy doesn't keep expanding, it will collapse." There you have it: growth for growth's sake, the philosophy of the cancer cell, as desert iconoclast Edward Abbey observed. The official paused a moment and then added with evangelical fervor, "The Lord put all those resources there for us to use!"

"But where does it end, are there no limits to consumption?" I asked. "It doesn't end!" he almost shouted, ending any further dialogue.

The township supervisor did have a point: we are riding on a tiger of consumption and it is hazardous to try to get off. However, if we cannot prevent "progress," can we at least redirect it? We have already drastically altered our natural environment to conform with the human agenda. How far are we willing to go in making sacrifices to appease the insatiable deity called *The Economy?* Is a still higher standard of living worth the cost to our planet? Those of us who cannot live happily without natural areas ask: can we try to curtail projects that further impoverish our natural heritage?

Glancing at my Muse, I see she is pouting and realize I have gotten off on a rant. I am sounding like a Luddite. I must not tarnish this autumn day and derail my pilgrimage. Seeing an opening in the traffic, I turn off the crowded highway and take a connecting street to County Road 492. Almost instantly I am riding along all by myself amidst wooded hills on a two-lane, twisting byway, with no neon hawkers or giant parking lots in sight.

Originally designed for the horse and buggy days—and, until the construction of re-routed U.S. 41, the main highway connecting Marquette and Negaunee—County Road 492 is a very pleasant drive. Dense maple and pine groves crowd close to the road, gradual hills offer scenic vistas and there are a number of challenging curves. It was these curves, and the many deadly accidents which occurred here, that prompted a county road crew foreman to make a momentous decision.

Picture it: a nice spring day in May 1917. William Skewis (a Cornish name which means, "sheltered place"), concerned about all the vehicular crashes caused by drivers rounding Dead Man's Curve on the wrong side of the road, takes a can of white paint and brushes an eight-inch line down the middle of the roadway.

Superior View Studio, Marquette, MI

Rounding a curve

"That'll keep them on their own side of the highway," he probably thought as he stood back to admire his work. Just then the Superintendent of the Marquette County Road Commission drives up, jumps out of his car and, after a long moment of astonishment, congratulates Bill on his initiative.

Kenneth Ingalls Sawyer (his mother's cousin was Laura Ingalls Wilder of *Little House on the Prairie* fame), an engineer and innovator, recognized instantly that the use of center lines on rural roads would reduce accidents. And there *was* an almost immediate decline in traffic mishaps on the winding road between Marquette and Negaunee. Sawyer cared more about results than personal credit for this very first use of white paint on highways in the Upper Peninsula and always shared the prestige for the innovation with his employee, Mr. Skewis. I stop to read again the historical plaque beside the road commemorating the event, and offer my appreciation to two thoughtful sons of the Upper Peninsula.

Later in his long career, Sawyer proposed a gasoline tax bill in the Michigan State Legislature to fund road building and maintenance. But the year was 1919, very early in Michigan's automotive history, and the engineer was literally laughed out of the House of Representatives. Five years later, he was vindicated when the bill passed. Sawyer also created Michigan's system of tourist roadside parks. One noon, so the story goes, he was sitting on a rock beside a U.P. highway eating his lunch when he got the idea of placing picnic tables at convenient spots for motorists. Now Michigan has one of the best, if not *the* best, system of roadside parks in the nation.

Sawyer was also a pioneer in the siting and building of airfields in the region. When the United States Air Force located a strategic air command facility in southern Marquette County in the 1950s, it was named K.I. Sawyer Air Force Base in honor of the forward-thinking engineer.

The road rises slightly as I reach the Morgan area, formerly the location of Morgan Heights Sanatorium, a chest hospital where, not so long ago, patients with tuberculosis were sequestered. Isolation, rest, exposure to sunshine and fresh air were the treatments of choice at that time. Built in 1911, with several later additions, the red brick buildings are located in a beautiful natural setting with tall white pines and granite hills. And, as the old sanatorium letterhead proclaimed, the facility was situated 1,300 feet above sea level and offered clear, invigorating air. As late as 1956, nineteen children were being treated at Morgan Heights.

The old sanatorium has been through several reincarnations over the years: a medical facility for the aged; a home for unwed mothers; and now a work site for a construction company. How fortunate we are that the incidence of tuberculosis is so low that we no longer need these former sanctuaries. Now that's a much better definition of progress!

Back on the road I slow down to inspect Morgan Creek. A short way upstream is Morgan Pond and the ghostly remains of Morgan, a once-thriving community where iron ore was smelted in the late nineteenth century. Who was Morgan and why does he have a creek, a pond and a town named for him?

Lewis Henry Morgan (1818-1881) was a Renaissance man: lawyer, anthropologist, wildlife biologist and developer of railroads and iron ore. He came to the Upper Peninsula originally to study beaver and wrote a definitive work, *The American Beaver and His Works*, which is still widely read and respected by scholars. Morgan liked what he saw in the Peninsula, particularly the burgeoning iron industry. In 1865, he built a blast furnace on the now-named Morgan Creek to smelt iron ore into blooms, called "pigs," which were hauled to the harbor in Marquette for shipment. To fire the furnace, charcoal was needed. Kilns shaped like beehives and looking like stone mushrooms were built throughout the forest. It takes thirty cords of wood to produce one thousand bushels of charcoal; that much charcoal will smelt five tons of ore. It doesn't take a rocket scientist to figure out what happened—the operation ran out of easily obtainable hardwood and the constant roar of the furnace ceased.

At one time, during its brief heyday, the town of Morgan boasted a population of three hundred workers and their families, several stores and its own post office.

The massive stone furnace is silent now; crumbling and in poor repair it sits brooding under a modern railroad trestle. When the ore trains rumble overhead, thousands of marble-sized iron pellets, the product of a new concentration process, cascade out of the shifting open cars and down on the old furnace and the roadway below.

Just across the creek to the north is an old field, where the pioneers cleared the land and erected their homes. The field is well on its way to becoming a maple and pine forest again, but stone foundations and holes where the cellars once were dug can still be seen. When I stand quietly in this old homesite, I can hear the wind keening around the corners of the primitive log cabins, the sound of men chopping and stacking wood and the shrill voices of children at play. Our heritage is close at hand in this region.

I go to the old town of Morgan often because, with the varied habitat, it's a great place to look for birds. In a prior lifetime I was a professor of speech pathology and I enjoyed every minute of my work with students and persons who spoke with slow and halting tongues. But I knew when I retired that I wanted, even needed, to do something very different with my life. When I left the university, my goal was to spend this last and best chapter of my life trying to connect people with nature. It seemed just natural that I would share my lifelong interest in birds.

One of my very favorite places to lead birdwatching expeditions is the ghost town of Morgan. With the creek, large pond, open field and dense forests, it is an ideal location for spotting a wide variety of birds. Last summer I led a large group of beginning birdwatchers who were attending an annual National Wildlife Foundation Nature Summit. It was a lively group of participants and they clearly enjoyed my freewheeling, joking style. As we were boarding the bus for the return trip to town from the old Morgan site, one elderly lady sidled up close to me and announced, "You look just like my third husband." Taken aback a bit, I searched for some response. "How many husbands have you had?" I asked finally. She moved even closer, looked searchingly at my face and said, "Two."

Already the morose mood of the shopping malls has lifted and now, to further raise my spirits, I need some *White Water*. No, I'm not referring to a float trip on a fast river but rather a distinctive Upper Peninsula treasure: *White Water*, a family folk band. Some family! Some band!

In 1985, Dean and Bette Premo, newly anointed with doctorates in environmental science, came to Amasa, a small village in the western Upper Peninsula.

They wanted to build a life and a livelihood in the area where the Premo forebears had pioneered for several generations.

"We wanted to watch over the home place," observed Dean, using a line from one of the family's repertoire of songs. Undaunted by all the possible pitfalls, the young Premo couple started an environmental consulting firm. They offered analytical chemistry, scientific consultation and environmental education. Working out of their home, they weathered some lean years and now White Water Associates, Inc., has its own spacious building, twenty employees and a national reputation.

We first met the Premo family through their reputation as music-makers extraordinaire. *White Water* concerts feature songs which reflect how we too feel about family, U.P. history and heritage, and love of the land. When they sing "Child of Mine," "Roseville Fair," or "Keweenaw Lights," Lynn and I experience a deep tug of emotion. Now that we have come to know the family better, their melodies resonate even deeper.

Dean Premo, scientist, woodworker, outdoorsman and keeper of local traditions, is the leader of the band. He plays guitar and sings lead in a clear tenor voice. I am one of Bette's secret admirers in the Upper Midwest. She plays a hammer dulcimer—one of many built by Dean—fiddle, mandolin, and banjo and is a lovely alto songster. But it is her dazzling smile which lights up even large concert halls and her lively personality that wins so many hearts.

Over the past several years, Lynn and I have had the privilege of watching the Premo children, Evan, seventeen, and Laurel, fourteen, mature into very accomplished musicians. Evan has played the bass since the age of eight. And does he play the bass! The sounds he coaxes out of that large instrument are phenomenal, so outstanding that he was selected to play with an orchestra touring the British Isles and in Carnegie Hall during the past year. And then there is Laurel. Lovely Laurel. She plays *everything*: fiddle, resonator guitar, mandolin, flute and a variety of percussion instruments. And she sings like a thrush in the morning.

So, those are the four performers of *White Water*, each talented, each enthusiastic about his or her art, each joyous in their lives. But when the family performs together, there is a beautiful blend of energy, talent and family affection that weaves a spell over those who attend their performances. Many of us in the Upper Peninsula have become *White Water* groupies.

Not only does the Premo family enrich my life in a myriad of ways, they also enthusiastically joined me on my ancestral pilgrimage—more about that later. Now, I insert a *White Water* cassette in my tape deck and cue up one of my favorite songs, "Friend for Life." I sing along with my own words in an uncertain baritone:

> *When you're down and out on a four-lane mess,*
> *your friend the song will be there with a kind caress.*

With apologies to song writers Bryan Bowers and Bill Danoff, I cruise down County Road 492 into downtown Negaunee, Iron Town, U.S.A. Here I shall pay my respects to the exact spot where iron ore was discovered in the Upper Peninsula.

Whenever I go through Negaunee, I always stop to look at Teal Lake. Since the highway travels right beside the lake for its two-mile length, I could just glance at it while driving past. But it is such a lovely body of water, so typical of the rock-rimmed lakes in the central and western Upper Peninsula, that I must linger and admire the morning light on the teal-colored water.

The lake was named by one A.B. Gray in 1846 while his crew was preparing a survey of the mineral claims in the region. From what I could discern, the name Teal refers not to a color but rather to two species of small ducks, blue-winged and green-winged teal, which Native Americans observed on the lake.

Teal Lake is ringed by granite outcroppings, particularly on its north and west borders. The Superior Peninsula is granite country. Almost everywhere one looks are rugged cliffs, weathered knobs, long shelves deeply grooved by glacial striations and gigantic boulders of the ancient rock. Granite is often found in association with water: inland lakes, particularly in the Michigamme Highlands, are often surrounded by sheer cliffs and flat slabs of it; most streams in the area tumble through or over it; most of the majestic Lake Superior shoreline is composed of it. It is this particular blend of rock, water and pines which give the Peninsula its unique charm, its heroic proportions and enduring character.

The granite of this region is pre-Cambrian in origin. In technical terms it is classified as the Southern Province of the Great Canadian or Laurentian Shield and is thought to be at least three-and-a-half billion years old. Hidden beneath the schist, granite and gneiss which comprise the shield is another substance—an element which had, and is still having, a profound impact on the development of the area. During the gestation of the earth mass, vast deposits of iron were laid down as chemical precipitates in the shallow waters of the bays and arms of the immense seas which covered this region in pre-Cambrian times. Since iron and oxygen commonly unite to form iron oxides, most of the iron was deposited as the minerals hematite, magnetite and goethite. The Marquette Iron Range was discovered quite by accident one day in the early fall of 1844, and the tide of speculators and miners pouring in to retrieve the treasure altered the Peninsula forever.

On September 19, 1844, William A. Burt and his party of surveyors were running a section line in the vicinity of Teal Lake when they noticed the compass fluctuating wildly. Puzzled when the compass refused to point true, the men split up and looked about; to their amazement, they found outcrops of raw iron ore in

White Water in concert

The Premo family: Bette, Dean, Evan and Laurel

Morgan furnace

Charcoal kiln at Morgan

every direction. Less than a year later, Philo Everett and a group of businessmen from Jackson, Michigan, arrived to search for the fabulous lode of iron ore. Their original intention had been to explore for copper in the Keweenaw Peninsula, but while resting at L'Anse they heard Louis Nolan, a part-Indian guide who had been with the Burt surveying party, talk about the mountain of iron ore in what is now the town of Negaunee.

At the mouth of the Carp River, near where the Marquette State Prison now stands, the party met a young Ojibwa woman, Tip-Kesa, who said that her uncle, a local chieftain, would show them the site of ore outcroppings. With Tip-Kesa as their guide, Everett and the Jackson party hiked up the Carp River Valley and found Marji-Gesick (Ojibwa for "Moving Day") encamped at Teal Lake. The Native Americans were frightened of the mountain of ore; its light reflected across the waters of the lake like a mirror and they referred to the area as the "mirrored wall of evil spirits." In spite of the superstition, Marji-Gesick led the Jackson party to an outcropping of iron ore under the roots of a fallen pine tree. In an amazing under-statement Philo Everett commented, "It is a mountain 150 feet high of solid ore, and looks as bright as a bar of iron just broken . . . what it will amount to I am not able to say." A month later the Jackson Mining Company was formed; the company secured mining permit #593 from the United States government which allocated one square mile of land—at $2.50 an acre. To secure their claim, the young company built six log houses and a barn; this marked the beginning of Negaunee.

When news of the discovery of rich iron ore deposits spread across the country, hundreds of speculators rushed to the area; within one year more than a hundred mining companies were formed. Unprepared for the rigors of the north, ill-equipped and underfinanced, most of the boom companies failed in the first year or two. But the Jackson Mine persisted and grew. At the outset, extraction of the ore was done in open pits carved into the hills where the iron was discovered; the drilling was accomplished by hand, using chisels and sledge hammers. The raw iron ore was laboriously carted by mule teams down to Marquette Harbor over a plank road. By 1857, railroads had been built for transporting the heavy ore. Some effort was made to process the ore into iron "blooms" (bars of pig iron, two feet long and four inches thick) near the mine sites. The Jackson forge was built in 1846 but the effort and expense to make the blooms was too costly. It became easier to ship the ore in bulk lake freighters to the furnaces of Gary, Cleveland and Pittsburgh where coal deposits were close at hand. Within a few years the outcrops of iron were depleted and the hard rock miners followed the veins of metal deep into the earth.

Investors made millions of dollars over several decades. Sadly, but typical of the treatment Native Americans received at the hands of Europeans, Marji-Gesick got only a piece of paper proclaiming that he had part ownership in the Jackson Mine.

Many years later, after extensive litigation, his descendants were awarded a niggardly cash settlement.

Negaunee is the very first iron mining city in the United States and, even though the halcyon years are long gone, the water tower still proclaims it Iron Town, U.S.A. The village was platted in 1865, but many years earlier Native Americans camped near here; instead of iron, these early residents used copper for making scrapers, knives and spear points. At first the city fathers wanted to name their town "Iron," but most people agreed that the Chippewa word, Nigani, which means "pioneer" or "first" would be more appropriate. European settlers changed the spelling later to Negaunee.

Parking by the Sundberg Block—"Built in 1890" says the weathered and cracking facade—I decide to walk on Iron Street, once a thriving business area, to get the feel of the town. Frankly, it looks like it has seen better days. Many of the stores are closed and the buildings look forlorn and weary. Most of the new business establishments are out on U.S. 41; here, the former commercial district is given over to bars and antique shops. The residents still care about the old town: there is a new community center, a well-equipped historical museum and one of the best public school systems in the region.

When I first explored the town in the 1960s, the business community seemed to be doing a lot better. Longtime residents encouraged us to visit Lowenstein's Department Store to get the flavor of an old-fashioned general merchandise store.

Sam Lowenstein started as a door-to-door peddler in the early 1900s. He lugged a huge suitcase over his shoulder and offered needles, thread and other sewing essentials to housewives in the comfort of their own homes. An energetic and frugal man, Lowenstein built a large dry goods store on thriving Iron Street. Sam Lowenstein had been gone for several years when Lynn and I visited the store. His two sisters, both quite elderly, ran the business. Entering Lowenstein's Department Store was like stepping back to 1925. The large ground floor display room had high ceilings, was furnished in dark wood and was barely illuminated. As we looked about at the merchandise on the counters, a thin, elderly woman appeared wraith-like out of the gloom and asked, "How may I help you?" Her voice was wistful, almost sepulcher in tone. While my wife tried on a dress, I wandered about the store, reveling in this commercial museum that reminded me so much of my childhood. When I returned from my brief tour, Lynn was inspecting herself in a dress clearly two sizes too large. The frail-looking clerk was positioned behind Lynn and, with a surprising show of strength, was pulling the blue shirtwaist dress tightly in the back.

"See how nicely it fits," she said hopefully, "Just a small adjustment and it will work fine."

The clerk was clearly disappointed when Lynn put the dress back on the rack and then made a small purchase. But l was ecstatic. The store still had an ancient system that whisked the bill and our money up to a mezzanine level where the purchase was recorded and the change counted. I watched in amazed childhood wonder as our clerk placed everything in a wire basket, rang a bell, and another elderly woman, obviously the other Lowenstein sister whom we had not noticed in the dark store, retrieved it using a pulley. The second sister, a carbon copy of our clerk, impaled the bill on a spindle and sent the basket whirring down with the change. The entire process took less than a minute, certainly far less time than I now wait impatiently for a clerk to click and look, click and look at the computerized register in a modern store.

I wanted to buy something else just to see the process repeated, but we had to go. Before I could return to Lowensteins, the store closed. That missed opportunity to witness the basket system in operation again is one of the small regrets of my life.

All this reminiscing has made me hungry and I decide to amble over to Beth's Kake Kreations, a small bakery on Jackson Street. I forgave Beth several years ago for the precious name she chose for her establishment because she makes pretty good bismarks. Since the bakery will close its doors for the last time this fall, I must get one more treat for the road.

For the past half-century I have been on a puerile quest to find the perfect bismark—raspberry if possible, but other flavors will serve. The search has been long, arduous and artery-clogging, but someone has to do it. Not long after we married, my wife and I took a long trip out west. In Bismarck, North Dakota—I bet you have already guessed what happened—I embarrassed my new bride and startled a sleepy waitress by announcing that finally I was going to have a bismark in Bismarck! You never know where a quest for bakeries will lead you.

In fact, my nose for saffron buns led me to John Johns, fellow Cornishman, retired iron miner and a longtime resident of Negaunee. While attending an open house for one of Lynn's colleagues, I noticed an elderly man standing on the fringe of a small conversation group. Although more diminutive, he looked startlingly like my grandfather: same wiry physique, Roman nose, icy-blue eyes and a stance that gave a suggestion of Celtic enthusiasm and merriment.

"You're a Cornishman, aren't you?" I asked rhetorically, without any preamble.

"Yes!" John responded immediately, "and you're also a Cousin Jack, I bet. I brought some saffron rolls to the party; let's go get one."

His voice offered just the hint of a Cornish moor and his smile was infectious. As we enjoyed saffron rolls and tea together, John told me his parents had come to the Upper Peninsula from Newquay, a village on the north coast of Cornwall. His father had been a miner and his mother ran a boarding house. John had followed his father into the mine and, after laboring underground for thirty-four years, retired to a life of travel and leisure. He retained his keen interest in iron mining history.

"Would you like to see the skip I've built?" John asked after I had pumped him for information about the industry.

"Well, sure . . . ah . . . ," I responded hesitantly, trying to remember the mining terminology my grandfather had shared so long ago.

"Good," he interrupted. We made a date for my visit. John seemed bemused that he was going to teach the professor about extracting iron ore.

When I arrived at his home on Ridge Street in Negaunee, John was primed for my lesson in mining; he had an old map of the Negaunee area, photographs of mining operations he had collected over many years and his wife, Alice, had a pasty for each of us in the oven. Happy to have a new audience, John launched into an iron ore treatise almost immediately after I entered the house.

"After iron ore was discovered by Burt, the old timers probed all over this area," he said, unfolding the map. "See, here's just a few of the old mines: Maas, Prince of Wales, Blue, Bunker Hill, Lucy, Hartford—most went bust right away."

"That's a lot of holes in the ground," I commented.

"Yep, this whole area is criss-crossed with underground diggings," John replied, "In fact, our house here had to be moved several years ago because the ground was caving under it."

Later, while we sorted through old black and white photographs, I paused at one particular picture. It showed two men with large hammers poised beside another worker holding a slender drill; the man holding the drill was smoking a pipe.

"That's called 'double jacking'," said John.

"How," I pondered aloud, "did the miner hold the chisel in his bare hands while those two other men alternated striking the head of the tool with sledge hammers?"

"With élan," John replied with a chuckle.

My eyebrows must have risen at his use of the word élan.

"Surprised, eh?" John said, "I know a bit of French, German, Italian and Finnish. We had people from all over working in the mines. It was really something, you know, to walk downtown in Negaunee then and hear all the different languages being spoken." He paused a moment, lost in memories, then chuckled and continued, "I remember a lad from Finland who only knew a few words of English. One day he told the crew boss: 'Them Cousin Jacks, they are sure smart. They're only here two days and they already speak English!'"

Later, when I inspected the working model of a mining skip John had built in his basement, I was astonished at the meticulous detail of his work. A *skip* is a

Double jacking at the Jackson Mine

hoisting device which raises the ore from deep in a mine shaft and deposits it into an ore car or a truck on the surface. John's miniature skip was very complete: it had an ore bucket—with real iron ore in a small pit—elaborate electronically-controlled pulley devices, lights and even a model train to transport the ore.

"What was your job in the mine?" I asked during our memorable pasty feast.

"I was an ore sampler," John said, "My job was to go down in different shafts, collect small bags of ore and then take them back to the lab to be tested."

John's work took him all over the iron range.

"Was it dangerous?" I inquired.

"Well, any underground work has its dangers," he said. "The only time I got into any serious trouble was when I was hoping to save some time and tried to crawl up a raise from one drift to another. To make a long story short, I got stuck—couldn't crawl forward or back up. I panicked a bit when my head lamp went dim. After I calmed down, I slowly dug little holes with the toes of my boots and, inch by inch, levered myself back down."

Sensing my uncertainty with the vocabulary of underground mining, John gave me a quick rundown of some commonly used terms:

shaft: the main hole dug into the earth; can be vertical or inclined; provides access for workers, the skip and various cables and hoses.

drift: every two hundred feet or so, tunnels are dug horizontally from the shaft; commonly ten feet high; allows for underground trains to transport ore to the shaft.

raise: an inclined tunnel running upward from one drift to another.

stope: a large underground opening or cavern in a drift which remains when ore is removed.

"Do you know what a 'sticking Tommy' is?" John asked.

I responded with hysterical laughter. "Someone named Thomas who sat in a puddle of Super Glue?" I volunteered between howls. Then I realized John wasn't making it up.

"Get serious, Professor," John said with mock severity, "There'll be a quiz later. A 'sticking Tommy' is a wire device to hold a candle on a miner's hat. There was a long point on the holder so the miner could stick it into a crevice when he started to work."

Consulting a large scrapbook, John showed me a list of some of the types of iron ore found in the Upper Peninsula mines:

magnetite: black crystalline iron oxide; tests at 72% iron

hematite: reddish-brown iron oxide; 70% iron

taconite: hard rock, quartz-rich, layered with bands of iron; 30% iron

All underground mining of iron ore was terminated in 1978 when the Mather B shaft in downtown Negaunee was closed. Now all ore extraction occurs in vast open pits. The raw ore is taken to huge processing plants for "benefication," a procedure which separates and concentrates the ore from waste rock.

"How does that process work?" I asked John as he put away his photographs.

"As I understand it," he said, "It works like this: first they crush the ore into smaller chunks; then it goes in a grinder and is ground into a fine powder; a magnet separates the iron from the rock; finally, the iron is pelletized by combining it with clay and rolling it in huge balling drums; then the pellets are dried in a kiln. The taconite pellets contain about 64% iron."

"You got in on some of the initial research on that benefication process, didn't you?" I inquired.

"Yep," John replied, "It's certainly easier this modern way, less dangerous, but . . ." John stared wistfully off into the distance for a long moment, then turned back, smiled and asked if I wanted to see some of his travel photographs.

John Johns and Alice had a long and pleasant retirement. John loved to travel and, not long after he stopped working, the couple took a once-in-a-lifetime trip around the world. When I asked them to describe some of the highlights of their journey, they mentioned Hong Kong, the Taj Mahal, Spain and Switzerland.

"But, the very best part of the trip? When the Northwest plane banked over Teal Lake and landed at the airport," John concluded. "And you know why?" He then told a story I have often repeated to people who ask why we live in the far north:

> On their world tour, the Johns visited Catholic churches wherever they happened to be. In a church in Sidney, Australia, they saw a white phone on the wall. A small sign read, "Direct Line to God—calls $10,000." A church in Budapest had a similar phone but this time the call cost $8,000. In Paris, the cost was $4,000. Finally, in New York City, a phone call direct to God cost $2,000. Upon returning home to Negaunee, John visited a local church to see what a phone call to God would cost. A sign proclaimed that such a call would be 10¢. John sought out the priest and asked why a call from Negaunee was only 10¢ when it cost so much more to call God from places overseas. The priest smiled and said, "Because from here, it's a local call."

FOUR

I t is now midmorning and I am driving up the hill beside Teal Lake on my way to Ishpeming, a twin city of sorts with Negaunee. Ishpeming is an Ojibwa word meaning "on high" but some of the locals insist the true meaning is "heaven" and then point down the hill to Negaunee with a smirk. A number of residents pronounce it "Ish*per*ming." When I first heard it, the added "r"sounded a bit quaint, but now I find it mildly annoying. One of our students who worked part-time for the city told me that two road workers once actually made a sign reading, "Ish*per*ming." A whimsical story—though probably not true.

Migrating waterfowl are gathering in the quiet bays. I see goldeneyes, mergansers and some others I can't identify at highway speed. A lone paddler in a yellow kayak skims along by the rock cliffs on the far side of the lake.

Ishpeming is another town that iron built. And still keeps it going—the offices of Cleveland Cliffs Iron Company are located here. I decide to take a brief detour off the highway into town and do a short walkabout. Time has been kinder to Ishpeming than Negaunee, although even a cursory glance suggests that the town had more life behind it than it does now. One large building, the former Gossard Lingerie Factory, attracts my interest because it provided a great source of entertainment for some of my former patients.

The lingerie factory's retail outlet was one of my favorite places to bring my patients, young men who stuttered, when they reached the point in speech therapy where they were attempting to transfer the skills they had learned in the speech clinic to real communicative situations. It may seem strange—-and probably reflects my zany sense of humor more than anything else—but Gossard's was an ideal place to begin, mainly because of the unusual nature of the transactions and the humor involved.

Humor is a very good antidote to the fear and anxiety at the core of most stuttering problems. One of the best tools in combating this fear is confronting the disfluent speech directly. We called this negative practice: purposely engaging in stuttering behavior when one does not need to. To most normal speakers, stuttering on purpose seems exceptionally weird.

Individuals who stutter must learn to tolerate some level of disfluent speech. Why? Because it helps to drain away fear and provides a lot of experience practicing the act of stuttering in a highly controlled manner. What have you got to hide if you are willing to stutter voluntarily? It's as simple as this: the more you stutter on purpose, the less you hold back; and the less you hold back, the less you stutter. Thus, it allows the person who stutters to be in command of the situation. One young university student put it this way:

> *"If I'm not afraid to stutter, then I won't be afraid I will stutter. Thus I have nothing to avoid or fear, and hence no stuttering to do."*

The therapist must be willing to show his client that he, too, is not afraid to stutter openly. This is an incredibly difficult concept for novice speech therapists to understand, let alone put into action. A wise mentor explained the rationale for the therapeutic procedure this way, with a parable:

> *A man falls into a pit and cannot find a way to crawl out. A physician passes by and the trapped man calls out for help. The doctor writes a prescription and lets it flutter down in the hole. Then an engineer walks past, responds to the appeal for assistance, draws a blueprint and drops it in the pit. A passing minister says a prayer and goes on his way. Finally, a friend comes by and jumps down into the hole with the trapped person. "What good is this going to do?" wails the man, "Now we are both trapped in here." "Yes," responds the friend, "but I know how to get out."*

Not long before the Gossard Factory shut down, four young men, ages nineteen to twenty-six, made the annual soiree to Ishpeming with me. Our goal was to simply inspect the merchandise until the clerks approached us and then use the situation for a speaking opportunity.

After we pawed through the brassieres and panties for several minutes, two clerks, both older ladies, approached our group. They had been watching the activity with some amusement and had smirks on their faces. When they asked, "Can we help you?", one of the bolder lads, who had been a leader throughout the group therapy regimen, smiled broadly and inquired, "W-w-w-where can w-we tttt-try these on?" The ladies recoiled at least three paces and looked at us with obvious alarm. After assuring the women that we meant no harm, the stutterers went on to explain what they were doing in therapy and why they were in the lingerie store. As almost always happened when we did these public forays, the clerks became intrigued in what the young men were doing, expressed admiration for their courage and we ended up having a lengthy and helpful exchange. My charges were ecstatic about their experience and insisted that we spend the day going around to other stores for more speaking opportunities. The therapist just smiled to himself and started the van.

In 1991, Charles Kuralt of CBS "On the Road" fame told an interviewer that John D. Voelker was "really about the nearest thing to a great man I've ever known." Lawyer, county prosecutor, Michigan Supreme Court Justice, trout fisherman and superb storyteller, Voelker was born and raised in Ishpeming. Although he had written earlier books, it was his narrative of a tavern murder in Big Bay, a hamlet north of Marquette, that brought him fame and fortune.

It all started with a sensational murder. Shortly after midnight on July 31, 1952, United States Army Lieutenant Coleman Peterson walked into the Lumberjack Tavern, a local watering hole, and emptied his pistol into owner-bartender Mike Chenoweth as he stood behind the bar. A burly former Michigan State trooper, Chenoweth (another Cornish name meaning "new house") fell, fatally wounded. The Lieutenant then returned to his trailer home in Perkins Park and surrendered to Deputy Fred Marsh.

Lieutenant Peterson's wife, Charlotte, had been at the Lumberjack earlier in the evening, drinking and playing shuffleboard. Chenoweth told her it was not safe to walk home because of bears and insisted on driving Charlotte to her trailer. Instead, he detoured onto a remote woods road where he assaulted and raped her. Mrs. Peterson escaped from Mike's car, fled to her trailer and told her husband of the assault.

Peterson was arrested and charged with murder. A former prosecuting attorney, John Voelker, was engaged to defend the Army officer. After a trial of only one week, the jury found Peterson "not guilty" by reason of temporary insanity, finding that he had been under the influence of an "irresistible impulse" when he killed Chenoweth. Three days later he was released from jail.

Under the pen name of Robert Traver, Voelker wrote *Anatomy of a Murder* and the rest, as they say, is history. The book was an instant success and was selected by the Book-of-the-Month Club in 1958. *Anatomy of a Murder* was on the national bestseller list for over a year.

Shortly thereafter, Otto Preminger decided to make a motion picture of the book and elected to film it on location in Marquette County. Hollywood stars Jimmy Stewart, Lee Remick, Eve Arden, Ben Gazarra, George C. Scott and Duke Ellington were selected for roles. The film was a great success and, although shot in black and white, still offers riveting entertainment.

The success of *Anatomy of a Murder* gave Voelker the freedom to pursue his literary interests. Resigning from the Michigan Supreme Court in 1959, he told the governor, "While other lawyers may write my opinions, they can scarcely write my books."

In later years, I would see Voelker in his old fishing car, laden with supplies, as he headed for his beloved Frenchman's Pond camp on the East Branch of the Escanaba River for an evening of fly-fishing. On rare occasions I would see him dining with his fishing cronies at some upscale eatery. One time, not long before he died, I introduced myself to the famous author in Marquette's Peter White Library where we both were browsing in the new book section. We chatted briefly and I was impressed with Voelker's graciousness and sardonic wit. Showing more temerity than good sense, I sent him a copy of an archery book I had written and was very touched by his supportive comments. Charles Kuralt was right: John Voelker *was* a great man, and certainly a favorite son of Ishpeming.

With great relief I pass the last bit of strip development at the west end of Ishpeming. Now I can see the contours of the land more clearly, the vast brightly-colored forest, the open spaces not yet impacted by the human agenda. For many of us who choose to live in these remote environs, natural landscapes are necessary for personal happiness and stability; they also promise new possibilities, new beginnings. I am reminded of something that expatriate poet Gertrude Stein wrote in 1936: "In the United States there is more open space where nobody is than where anybody is. That is what makes . . . America what it is." Would she say that today?

No matter. I am out of town and in a burst of exuberance I shout, "Hoka Hey! It is a good day to drive," startling my Muse almost off her perch on the dashboard. I don't even mind gliding past the ghostly remnants of old mining locations—Diorite, Clarksburg, Humboldt. (Here's an interesting fact about this ghost town, in case you are ever on some trivia show: In the 1880s, Thomas Edison did some pioneer "benefication" experiments here with low-grade iron ore. Although not successful, or even needed then with the seemingly unlimited supply of rich ore, this initial research contributed to new efforts in the next century). Glad to be at highway speed, the Silver Shrike puts his hood down and aims for the village of Champion where I have a rendezvous with the late Drs. Van Riper.

It is difficult to rein in the Silver Shrike and we careen over and down a steep hill into Champion at warp speed. Established as a mining location in 1865 by the Oliver Mining Company, the village reached, its zenith with a population of 2,500 in the early 1900s. The mine has been closed for a long time, and now the small town sleeps beside the highway. But I will stop here, I must stop here, and pay my respects to the Drs. Van Riper.

Turning left off U.S. 41 at the lone blinker light, I make my way up a hill past the large old yellow brick high school and pause in a moment of reverence in front of the Van Riper ancestral home. When my students and I went on speech therapy field trips around the Upper Peninsula, I always took them up this hill and stopped by this two-story colonial home. It was here, I pointed out, that our profession had its origin. "We are here today," I told them, "because Charles Van Riper was there yesterday."

A former stutterer and the first Ph.D. trained in the fledgling field of speech pathology, Dr. Van, as so many of his former students lovingly referred to him, established a soon-to-be-renowned speech clinic and training program in 1936 at Western Michigan College in Kalamazoo. He told me later that it was as close as he could get at that time to Champion and his beloved Upper Peninsula. Using all of his prodigious creative energy, Van founded a new profession. He traveled widely demonstrating and explaining the new field, worked with hundreds of patients, particularly stutterers, and trained several generations of professionals who then went forth with great zeal to emulate their mentor all over the nation. In his "spare time," he wrote the textbooks which summarized what was known in speech pathology. His book, *Speech Correction: An Introduction to Speech Pathology and Audiology*, became a classic and in its 10th edition is still the most popular introductory text in the field.

Charles Van Riper was a fabulous human being. He nurtured, inspired and sometimes infuriated hundreds of students and speech therapy clients during his long tenure as professor and therapist. He had an uncanny ability to intuit exactly what a particular individual needed at a particular moment. Sometimes it was a figurative kick in the pants; at others, a fatherly embrace. Dr. Van helped me immensely with my own stuttering problem and followed my academic career with interest and support. Once, when I was at a confusing crossroad in my career as a university teacher, he advised me to accept a position at a small college in Marquette if I wanted to live well. I did and I have. Later, he coaxed me into writing a textbook in a hitherto neglected aspect of speech pathology. Finally, near the end of my own academic tenure, Van invited me to coauthor two revisions of his legendary introductory text.

In later years, Dr. Van invited us to his hideaway north of Champion to hunt, fish and roam the woods. He did not invite many to his remote cabin but he loved my wife and twin daughters and insisted we use the new lovingly-crafted log cabin he had built for his elderly father, Dr. Paul Van Riper. When I asked Van about his father, he said simply that he was an easy man to admire, but a hard man to love. I decided that I had to meet the elder Dr. Van Riper and see for myself.

Old Doc Van, as everyone called him, was a much-beloved legend in the

Champion area. Small wonder, since during his long tenure as a country physician he had attended the birth of most of the local residents. When I went to see him, under the pretext of a cold, he was, at age ninety, still carrying on a limited medical practice. Almost immediately I could see what my mentor had meant about his father. His greeting was brusque, almost curt, as he led me into his den just off the parlor. A short, dignified-looking elderly man, he was dressed in a white shirt, blue tie, dark trousers and gray cardigan sweater. He sat down, lit his pipe, leaned back precariously in a creaky wooden swivel chair and surveyed me critically.

As I introduced myself, he interrupted and said gruffly, "Speak up now, I'm kinda deaf." Somewhat ill at ease, I talked too much, found myself babbling on about my Cornish forebears, how much I admired his son and my new position in speech pathology at Northern Michigan University.

"Oh," Doc Van interrupted bluntly, "You're not a real doctor, you're one of those 'talking kind,' like my son, Charles."

When I finally got around to telling him about my head cold, the purpose of my visit, the old physician interrupted again. "Well, a cold's not much of a problem really, is it? If I treat it, you get better in seven days. If not, it takes a week. So, take your pick."

I hesitated. "Oh, hell, as long as you're here, let's take a look at you," he said. Muttering something to himself, Doc Van listened to my chest, looked in my throat and took my temperature.

"You're as healthy as a horse, young man." he said. "But, here, if it will make you feel better, here's some pills you can take for five days. What color do you like? I have pink, blue, yellow and white. They're all the same anyway."

I smiled and took pink. "How much is your fee?" I asked.

"Forget it," he replied, "Too damn much paperwork anyway. It's on the house."

As I turned to leave, Doc Van called me back. I thought he had changed his mind about a bill for services and took out my wallet.

"No, put away your bloody wallet," he said, "You seem like a nice young man, a bit verbose, but nice. I want to give you some free advice that Ol' Doc George Beech, my predecessor on this job, gave me when I arrived here. 1901, I believe. Anyway, here's what Doc Beech told me: 'Don't ever change your diagnosis because the patient will lose faith in you, and believing in the doctor is half the cure.'"

Doc Van leaned back in his creaky chair and chuckled. "Wouldn't you know," he continued, "One of the very first patients I saw, a man of forty or so, came in with stomach complaints. Well, I looked him over real good, pressed his abdomen, did everything you could those days. Finally, I told the patient he was suffering from locked bowels and gave him a laxative. The guy looked at me real funny and then said, 'Well, Doc Van, I don't know how that can be. You see, I've had diarrhea for the last week!' What could I say? Thinking quickly, I replied, Well that may be so, but you still have locked bowels—they are locked in the open position."

Heading west out of Champion, I chuckle once again at Old Doc Van's pithy tale of the locked bowels. I told that story to my novice speech therapists many, many times and they always got a kick out of it. And learned from it, too. As I go past Van Riper State Park, a beautiful camping and recreational site on the east end of Lake Michigamme named for Paul Van Riper, I whisper my thanks to both the doctors for many services rendered.

Yet my mission here is not complete. The real Van Riper spirit dwells, I believe, not in the village but north at three lovely rock-rimmed lakes. So I turn off the highway and drive slowly up the Peshekee Grade, a twisting narrow strip of macadam that crosses the Peshekee River several times as it winds north into the Michigamme Highlands.

Near here, in 1987 and again in 1989, the Michigan Department of Natural Resources reintroduced moose to the area; since it is the annual mating season, I may be lucky enough to see one. Further north on the Grade is the McCormick Wilderness Tract, twenty-seven square miles of dense forests, granite outcrops, rushing streams and pristine lakes. Once owned by Cyrus H. McCormick, inventor of the reaper, and then his descendants, the handsome, virile land is now part of the Ottawa National Forest, one of two national forests in the Superior Peninsula.

There are modern pictographs on the dark rock outcrops beside the road. Some latter-day traveler wants the world to know that "Arnie loves Megan." Another spray-painted message announces that "Mergatroid" passed by here in 1997. A road sign is ventilated with nine bullet holes; no doubt it served as a target of opportunity for some disgruntled hunter or a wayward youth with too much disposable income.

Who are these people with the cans of paint and firearms? Do they live nearby or are they fugitives from large cities in southern Michigan and other states? Are they the sort of individuals who go ballistic in traffic or are committed to a life of random violence? Has Arnie been married three times but still has the same in-laws? Is Mergatroid the type of angry and lawless person who might accost you in the forest like a scene from *Deliverance*? Where, I wonder, but only briefly, are these people right now?

Just after the second bridge over the Peshekee River, I turn onto the Wildcat Road, a rough dirt lane snaking through the forest. Although the Silver Shrike dislikes taking these digressions from our main objective, when I shift into four-wheel drive, he leans into a bumpy hill, relishing the opportunity to flex his transfer case, his heavy-duty springs and show his back road skills.

Lon Emerick

Leopold Lake

Golden leaves

Shortly we bounce up to the gate that guards the Van Riper Shangri-la. Although I know how to open the barrier, on this mission I must approach slowly, respectfully and on foot. As I near the hand-hewn, meticulously-crafted log cabin beside the largest of the Leopold Lakes, the splendor of the spot overwhelms me. Sitting on a huge pine stump on which my speech therapy mentor used to dream countless outdoor fires, I admire the autumn colors ringing the lake and reflected in the water—a rich double blessing.

Then, as if by some cosmic magic, leaves begin to fall all around and on me. Stunned by the blessing of the golden leafy shower, I sit in reverent awe. Remembering an old legend—that a person will have one month of good luck in the new year for each leaf caught in midair as it falls—I run from place to place with outstretched hands until I have a year's supply of good fortune in the form of leafy bits of sunshine.

Exhilarated, I resume my seat on the stump to soak in the marvel of the morning. Just then, one last yellow maple leaf spirals down and lands softly on my head. A golden crown for me on a wooden throne. As I sit there contemplating this wonder, I think that I am distinguished more by this blessing of a simple yellow leaf than I would be by all the jewels of the British royalty. I wear the leaf all the way back to my truck.

FIVE

Hill after hill as far as I can see and beyond, all decorated in a rollicking display of autumn color. Lake Michigamme, at six miles long one of the largest inland lakes in the region, is on my left and keeps me company all the way to the next wee village, appropriately named Michigamme. Like most towns in this part of the Peninsula, Michigamme, too, was born as an iron mining location. It now has a precarious new life catering to summer visitors.

Just west of here, near a blip along the highway with a pretentious name, Imperial Heights, is a defunct iron mine that Henry Ford the Elder bought in 1920. Ford poured huge amounts of money into the failed shaft and finally abandoned it in 1926. Old Henry disliked having to rely upon the uncertainties of suppliers and was desperate to have his own sources for steel and wood to build his flivvers. The Ford dollar-shaped footprints can be found all over the Upper Peninsula and, not too far down the road, I shall run across his spoor again.

Several other wealthy men were charmed and proceeded to purchase large chunks of this remote and wondrous region for their personal pleasure. Just north of here, not far from the regal-sounding Imperial Heights, is Craig Lake State Park, 6,900 acres of lakes, ponds and dense forests. In the early 1950s, Fred Miller of the Miller Brewing Company purchased a tract of land for a fishing and hunting retreat and a place to entertain business associates. A lodge and a cabin were built. There are six lakes in the area and Miller named three of them for his children—Craig, Teddy and Clair. In celebration of the Miller Brewing Company, and all the beer that funded the purchase of the land, one was named Highlife Lake.

When Miller and one of his sons were killed in a plane crash, the property was sold to a logging company. The State of Michigan acquired the land in 1966. Craig Lake State Park is now a designated wilderness; no hunting is permitted and access is only by non-motorized means. We have camped, fished and hiked many times here, but today I will just wave at the primitive access road and, like Lewis and Clark, proceed on. Now I am in a region of vast boreal bogs, the home of tamarack trees.

The tamarack, *Larix laricine*, also called larch, is a tree that has an identity crisis: it can't seem to make up its mind if it's a conifer or a deciduous tree. It is, in fact, the only conifer that sheds its needles in autumn. For a brief interval after the maples, birches and aspens have dropped their many-splendored raiment, tamaracks put on quite a show. Every wetland is dotted with a display of understated dark gold; Sigurd Olson, fabled advocate of the Boundary Waters of Minnesota and lyrical defender of all things wild, called it "smoky gold."

Not a very large tree, the tamarack grows slowly in wet muskeg in close company with sphagnum moss, leatherleaf, and, in some cases, black spruce. This is an ideal habitat for boreal chickadees, gray jays, red crossbills and other far northern species of birds. The wood of tamarack is close-grained, hard and very strong. Those that have died remain standing for a long time. Native Americans showed Europeans that the resin from tamaracks was good for healing wounds. Unfortunately, much like the lamprey, zebra mussel and other undesirable species, the larch sawfly was introduced to North America from Europe in 1853. The larvae of the sawfly devastated entire stands of tamarack, killing almost all the old-growth trees.

The forest of tamarack I pass now is still wearing its soft lacy green needles. Cumulus clouds are building in the western sky, but they look benign and my spirits are buoyant as I reach the small resort community of Three Lakes.

There are indeed three lakes here, Beaufort, George and Ruth, and the highway offers a superb view of each of them glinting in the late morning sun. I will stop at the public access to Ruth Lake and remember years so long ago when we explored the Upper Peninsula with our twin daughters.

When you really get to know and come to love the place where you live, every bit of its geography is invested with memories. Every turn in the path evokes the thought "This is where . . ." Starting when Mary and Lynn were quite young, we took them camping, canoeing and exploring all over this beautiful and rugged land. What a magical time we had roaming around the far reaches of our native valley. We didn't know it then, but the seeds planted during those adventures would grow and blossom many years later in the girls' choice of careers in the out-of-doors.

One late spring day during one of our sojourns, we chanced to stop at Lake Ruth for a picnic and possibly an early season swim. The water was still too cold, but Lynn and Mary combed the beach for treasures, mementoes of our adventures they kept in a small box for later inspection. Mary picked up a rock, looked at it with some surprise, and then, unaccountably, tossed it into the lake. Instantly she realized what she had done. "It was the prettiest rock in the world," she lamented. We all searched in the icy water for this prettiest of rocks but, much to Mary's disappointment, we failed to find it. Often when I pass this way, I stop and search for this most beautiful of all rocks, not in hopes of ever finding it, but to remember those two young girls eagerly exploring their world.

Resuming my journey, I think about our lovely, talented daughters, now experienced and respected professionals. Mary serves as a wilderness specialist with the

Forest Service in Sitka, Alaska; Lynn is the fire suppression manager at Grand Canyon National Park, North Rim. Even though they are far away today, they are here in my spirit on this pilgrimage to find our Cornish ancestors.

Looking down the highway, I spot three large black birds picking enthusiastically at a flattened carcass. The overall size and formidable beak tell me that they are northern ravens. Waiting until the last second, they take a hop to get airborne and as they whirl overhead, their wedge-shaped tails confirm the identification. I have admired these intelligent scavengers for many years but not as much as Bernd Heinrich who has written (among others) two fascinating books about ravens: *Ravens in Winter* and *Mind of the Raven*. Lost in thought about ravens, I find myself ten miles down the road and almost to my next stop, Canyon Falls on the Sturgeon River.

There are very few canyons in the Superior Peninsula, and certainly nothing on the scale of those found in Arizona, Utah, Montana or other western states. But here, where the Sturgeon River flows through a narrow, steep-walled rock corridor, we have a gorge that is thrilling enough, it will serve.

No one is in the parking lot when I pull in, and, with great anticipation, I hurry down the trail to the noisy falls. We have had rain this past week and the river is dancing and surging down through its rocky margins. Pine, maple and cedar trees crowd close to the edge of the gorge and I slip quietly through the dense forest to find my favorite vantage point, a flat rock overlooking the falls. Although I don't really have time today for a lengthy communion in this magic spot, I find, as always, that I am mesmerized by the rushing water. Is there any feature of nature more appealing than moving water?

Such moments in nature are best experienced, I think, by trying to abandon language and allowing events to pass over us as raw sensations. I focus on my senses: feeling the soft breeze and mist on my face, hearing the thunder of the river, seeing the small rainbow forming near the base of the falls, and smelling the clean, elemental aroma of aerated water. If you have tried to achieve this zero-symbol state, you know how difficult it is to stop the dance of words across your cerebral cortex. I am told that Zen masters can extend their perception without language intervening for thirty seconds, sometimes even longer. Most of the rest of us are lucky to reach ten seconds without some interpretive thought intruding.

Language is such a wonderful human accomplishment, and I spent a professional lifetime helping others grasp the magic of words. But, as with any great asset, our proclivity for constant verbalization can also be a liability. It is good to remind ourselves that words are metaphors, substitutes for reality, convenient shorthand maps of our perceptual territory. What we *call* things are not the things.

Sturgeon River Gorge

Lon Emerick

Canyon Falls

Lon Emerick

"River, take me along"

Well, I got carried away there and am going on like some New Age guru. Maybe I should simply resort to poetry, or even better, verse put to music to reflect what passed through my mind on the rock perch beside Canyon Falls:

"River, take me along, in your sunshine
sing me your song
Ever moving and winding and free,
You rolling old river, you changing old river
*Let's you and me river run down to the sea." ***

So, in a state of grace from moving water, I retrace my steps to the Silver Shrike and am unprepared for the jarring encounter that awaits me at the parking lot. Pulled in lengthwise across several parallel parking slots is an immense motor home. Tethered behind the metal and glass behemoth like a baby elephant is a red Ford Escort. A portly man dressed in a tan jumpsuit is assembling what seems to be a television satellite dish.

"Howdy!" he calls loudly as I approach, "Mother wants to watch Oprah." He continues between grunts, "And I need to check out how our investments are doing on CNN."

Transfixed in a spasm of mental dissonance, I pause in midstride. Taking that as a sign of interest, the man approaches with an outstretched hand.

"Floyd Gertz is my name, and RVin' is my game," he announces. "Say," he asks, "you been to the falls?" Not waiting for my reply, he continues, "Is it worth the walk?"

What can I say? I despise the question—it is often asked rhetorically—because the implication is that the value of the natural world is measured by human convenience. I stand stiffly like an ungulate caught in car headlights and inspect my unexpected interlocutor. Floyd Gertz is a man of about sixty, of average height, with a vast abdomen straining to be free from the full length zipper of his jumpsuit. A blue baseball cap proclaiming, "Retired, No Boss, No Mondays, No Hassle, No Money" adorns his head.

Ignoring my catatonic confusion and his unanswered question—clearly he was not going to walk the half-mile to the falls anyway—Floyd insists I come inside so he can show me around his new motor home.

"It's the latest Itasca Suncruiser," he says expansively, "the coach is thirty-seven feet, five inches long, and it's got a V-10 engine and automatic transmission. See, it's even got a slideout for more room."

---

*Bill Staines, *River*, Red House Records, Inc. P. O. Box 4044, St. Paul, MN 55104, by permission.

Whatever possesses me to continue in this demonstration of how some older Americans take all their possessions on the highway, I don't know. But now I am committed and can think of no graceful way to flee.

"Yep," Floyd drones on, "I'm taking Mother to Arizona for the winter. We have a spot on the concrete reserved in Quartzite. Lots of RVers come there. We have lapidary, bingo, bridge tournaments. It's neat. Come on in and meet Mother—you can check out the inside."

With some reluctance I enter the Gertz palace on wheels.

"Blanche," Floyd says, "This guy's a real Yooper, walked all the way to the falls." Turning to me, Floyd asks, "What's your name again?"

"Ed Abbey," I say, using the name of my favorite iconoclast and eco-warrior in a small bit of humor. Floyd gives no indication that he's aware of the irony. Neither does Blanche.

Blanche sits at a table playing solitaire. She is chubby, has frizzy auburn hair, and wears a green velour sweatsuit which obviously has never seen a single molecule of perspiration. A box of Whitman Sampler chocolates lies open on the table and a white toy poodle sits on her lap.

"Pleased to meet you, I'm sure," Blanche says glancing up briefly and then returning to her card game. "Oh, this is Suzie," she adds, nodding at the dog. Suzie has a scarlet bow entwined in a tuft of hair on her head. It seems to me the poodle knows how ridiculous she looks because she fixes me with limpid dark eyes and growls, as if to say, "Don't even think about it, Buster, or I'll bite your ankle."

"She won't bite," Blanche says and then adds, "Floyd, is the dish ready? I don't want to miss Oprah, you know."

"Yeh, yeh," Floyd responds, "I just want to show Ed here the inside of our coach."

The motor home is lavish by any standards of American conspicuous consumption. There is a 25-inch color TV, chrome light fixtures, thermal-insulated windows, a built-in oven and microwave, a portable washer/dryer combination and much more. Midway through the tour my mind closes to the opulence and, when Floyd pauses for my expected expression of awe and admiration, I simply look at him in astonishment. Finally, I say, "All the comforts of home, eh?"

Floyd must have detected the note of sarcasm in my voice because he looks at me sharply and responds, "Nothing wrong with that." He pauses and then advises, "You should get yourself one of these coaches, it sure beats staying up here in the sticks all winter."

While I am not about to shepherd around a huge "pig rig," as my park and forest ranger daughters and their colleagues call gas-guzzling recreational vehicles, I must confess I did entertain the notion of being a snowbird at one time. A restless peregrination around the nation in a box of metal and glass held little appeal, but I did think it might be pleasant to spend winters in Arizona. After teaching for a semester at Northern Arizona University in Flagstaff, I became fascinated with the southwest: the blend of Native, Hispanic and Anglo cultures, the intriguing feel of the desert, the red rock country, the vast forests of ponderosa pines. So one year after I retired from teaching, with some reluctance on the part of my Life Partner, we spent a month in Prescott.

Prescott is located in north central Arizona. A small town—at least it was before being recognized in a national magazine as *the* place to retire—it is situated in the Bradshaw Mountains surrounded by the Prescott National Forest. It has a beautiful city square, streets lined with historic homes and, most important to us, many opportunities to wander. Close to the Grand Canyon, the red rock canyons of Sedona and the Sonoran desert, it should have been an idyllic respite. But I soon became disenchanted and melancholy.

Instead of Lynn and Lon in our home place, where we know and are known, we had joined the flock of mature individuals cluttering up the town. Most of our conversations with longtime residents began with the nervous inquiry: "Are you planning to move here?" Even in local stores we noted posters which read: "If the person in the car ahead of you is elderly, and so is the driver in the car behind you, you must be in Prescott." Lynn and I found ourselves making pre-emptive strikes in our encounters with locals, telling everyone we met that we were *not* moving to Prescott.

Have you ever noted that, when several members of one particular age group are clustered together, the worst behavioral traits seem to emerge? The situation becomes what social psychologists call a "behavioral sink." Whenever we went to restaurants, especially during the "early bird" hours, we overheard groups of retirees talking about medications, surgery, arthritis, even serious discussions of irregularity. Lamenting the untoward behavior of young people today and reviewing financial matters were also frequent topics of conversation. But the thing that got to me most of all was the way many people spent their days. Lacking any meaningful connection to the local community, many of our age cohorts resorted to filling their days with "planned activities." It seemed to me that many of the snowbirds were simply perched in Prescott for the season, employing shallow diversions such as golf, card playing, shopping and bingo to pass the time.

I felt uprooted, fragmented, a noncitizen. There was no continuity to the past, no personal landmarks, no sense of identity with a community. And my connection to the land, to my home place, was severed.

Thus it is that I am a determined homebody and, when away from this Superior Peninsula for very long, a morose sojourner. Like my literary mentor Thoreau did in Concord, I travel extensively in my own native valley. Oh, I know that those who are rooted deeply in place are sometimes viewed as vegetative, nonadventurous, even stuck-in-a-rut. Moving along seems to suggest moving up and the wanderer is somehow romantic, inspiring, footloose and fancy free. Perhaps. Is it not better, more deeply satisfying, to live in one place and really know it than to have been a visitor in a score or more? Some are born to a landscape and bloom wonderfully where they are planted. Others, pilgrims like myself, eschew the temporary titillations of a migratory existence and search for their Eden. Some of us are lucky enough to find it. St. Brigit of Ireland challenged a group of restless seekers with this short verse:

> *Tis labor great and profit small*
> *To go to Rome;*
> *Thou wilt not find the king at all*
> *Unless thou find him first at home.*

Henry Ford tried to buy himself an Eden just down the road from Canyon Falls where the Plumbago Creek crosses U.S. Highway 41. Mr. Ford liked coming to the sparsely populated upper Peninsula to get away from the traffic and pollution around the industrial centers in Detroit. I'm not sure he ever saw the connection between his mass production of automobiles and the confusion and congestion he fled. "What about creating a model community in an isolated northwoods area?" Ford thought. Here, he could demonstrate the simple values and lifestyle of an earlier era.

Starting in 1935, Ford built a town, Alberta, named for a daughter of his Upper Peninsula chief of operations. He visualized a self-sufficient village based upon the production of lumber (which he needed for making his cars) and agriculture. Eventually there were twelve houses, two schools and a huge steam-powered sawmill constructed near the Plumbago. In a short time, thirty families moved into Alberta.

Alas, it was not to be an idyllic village for very long. Ford's quixotic experiment to revert to a simpler time was doomed to failure. Henry Ford had let the genie out of the assembly plant and the simple, rural, self-sustaining lifestyle rapidly became extinct. In 1954, the Ford Motor Company gave the entire village and sawmill to Michigan Technological University and it was run as a milling operation for a short time. Now the village is a teaching facility, visitor and conference center.

I take a brief stroll around Alberta to try to get a feel of the place, but it seems so clean and contemporary that I can't imagine what it was like in 1936. Wandering over to the old sawmill, I think of all the trees that were cut to become frames, floor-boards and decorative wooden sides for Mr. Ford's vehicles. It took 250 board feet of lumber to build a car. Perhaps I am being an environmental curmudgeon. After all, I live in a log home and use wood products. But for anyone who reviews the history of logging in the Upper Peninsula, there can be no denying the rapacious and thoughtless way the region was stripped of its native pine.

The Europeans discovered a vast forest when they came to the Upper Peninsula. It must have been a marvel to behold, but to most settlers it was a dark, foreboding realm, a hiding place of savages and formidable wild creatures. A few saw a fortune to be made and launched a blitzkrieg of logging. These early lumber barons even invoked divine providence to rationalize the speed and completeness with which they felled the tall pines: "God has not given us these trees to simply watch them fall and decay," they said piously while pocketing large sums of money. It was thought the pine would last forever, but most was gone in twenty-five years; now there are only a few remnants of old growth pine still standing on the Peninsula.

Three species of pine are native to this region: jack, red and white, and each has a distinctive personality. My colleagues in the Biology Department at the University roll their eyes and mutter something about quaint anthropomorphism when I say that but, not being limited by Linnaeus, I persist. Besides, the trees and I have a more personal and friendly relationship, one that nurtures me and, I think, may be pleasing to the trees as well.

The smallest of the three pines, rarely growing more than fifty to sixty feet, the **jack pine** has a ragged, twisted appearance. Some call it the "poor man's pine." It does seem impoverished when compared to the lofty white or red pine. Furthermore, it likes to grow in large tracts on poor, sandy soil; the extensive stands are often called "plains" or, the pejorative term, "barrens."

Even the needles, two to a cluster, are twisted and prickly to the touch. Jack pine cones are hard and twisted, too. These small cones are tightly sealed with resin and only open to release their seeds in intense heat, as found in a forest fire. Since it requires fire to reproduce, the jack pine is a pioneer species, a tree first to colonize after a conflagration.

What good is it anyway? More than a decade ago I was privileged to serve on the board of the Sigurd Olson Institute in Ashland, Wisconsin. I was astounded, then outraged, when a longtime member of the board asked the assembled group—in reference to a flock of crows, which he complained woke him too early in the morning—"What good are crows, anyway?" Can you believe it? In a quarterly meeting of the Sigurd Olson Institute! I interrupted a wildlife biologist from the Apostle Islands National Lakeshore, who was attempting to offer a rational response, turned to the rhetorical questioner and blurted, "For that matter, what good are you?"

Not smart. But then I can blame it on my volatile Celtic ancestors. It turned out that the man who disliked the crow alarm clock was a wealthy banker and a generous contributor to the Institute. So my curt comeback hung on the air like a flatus in a cathedral. No one said anything when a short time later I quietly resigned from the board.

So, what good is the jack pine anyway? I'll tell you. The Bird of Fire, the Kirtland's warbler, sometimes also called the jack pine warbler, requires the small pine to nest and reproduce. An endangered and very rare species of bird, the Kirtland's warbler has very narrow requirements for its survival: it builds its nest on the ground at the base of five-to-twenty-year-old jack pines. The lower branches of the pines provide protection from predators and the elements. This gorgeous small, yellow, dark gray and black bird with the lively song nests primarily in four counties in the Lower Peninsula of Michigan. I say primarily because, in the past few years, nesting Kirtland's warblers have been documented in several counties of the Superior Peninsula, including my home township. May his tribe increase!

The jack pine plains are also the home of a remarkable wild fruit. The most prolific and most sought-after berry, and the one most symbolic of the north, is the blueberry. It is a hardy plant and grows abundantly in well-drained, sandy soil. It is one of summer's simple pleasures to hear blueberries drum into a metal container and watch the blue mound grow. To me, blueberries are the very essence of a northern summer: the small sweet morsels remind me of accumulated sunshine, nature's little beads of delicious warmth. Anyone who has enjoyed wild blueberry pancakes, muffins, pies or tarts knows what I mean.

Unlike the gnarled, straggly jack pine, the **red pine** is a handsome and stately tree. It grows tall, as high as eighty or even a hundred feet, and ramrod straight. Dressed in its reddish-gray, papery bark, it looks quite formal and reserved. Despite its size, the red pine has small cones; its long sharp needles are in clusters of two. Early settlers thought it looked a lot like an evergreen tree in Europe and called it Norway pine; the inappropriate label still lingers.

Before lumbering began on such a large scale, red pine made up only 15% of the native forest in the Upper Peninsula. Then timbermen noticed that red pine grows rapidly and makes nice straight saw logs, so it was planted extensively in reforestation. After clear-cutting an area, logging companies planted row-upon-straight-row of red pine. The result is an easy-to-harvest tree plantation, but not a forest. In fact, those stands of even-growth red pine—and we have a lot of them in our national forests—tend to be biological deserts. They provide a poor habitat for birds and other wildlife.

Some trees are so distinctive in shape that even observers with no knowledge of forestry can identify them. Look on the horizon: there, rising above other pines, are

Lon Emerick

White pine, the Upper Peninsula's signature tree

Lon Emerick

Smoky Gold—Tamarack in Autumn

graceful, plume-like branches which extend horizontally and then angle upward toward the sky. To me, it seems as if the **white pine** is raising its wooden arms upward in exultation.

Pinus strobus. Eastern white pine, king of the pines, Michigan's state tree. The largest conifer growing in the eastern part of North America, the white pine has had a long and sometimes uneasy interaction with civilization.

In 1605, Captain George Weymouth of the British Royal Navy eased his ship up several rivers along the coast of what was to become the state of Maine. Weymouth and his men were amazed at the pines they saw: tall, straight and growing in groves so thick they blotted out the sunlight. When they explored further, they found that the dense foliage of the pines allowed no underbrush to grow and the sailors walked about in perpetual purple twilight. Weymouth cut some of the pine for ships' masts, gathered some cones to send back to England (they did not grow) and claimed these magnificent trees for the crown.

The stands of white pine appeared to be endless—pioneers later discovered they extended all the way to northern Minnesota and south into the Appalachian Mountains. What to do with this seemingly inexhaustible bounty? Why, cut them down, of course. As early as 1623, settlers were felling the huge pines and selling them abroad. Would-be farmers treated the trees as large weeds and set about slashing and burning to open the land for their crops. I suppose we should not be surprised by the immigrants' choices: they had to wrest a living from this new continent and they came from a land which had been all but denuded of its native forests by centuries of human impact.

The English authorities took umbrage at the settlers' casual harvesting of the king's pines. In order to stop the practice, they branded the largest white pines with a royal crest—in the shape of a broad red arrow—to remind would-be axemen that these huge trees belonged to the crown. The colonists thumbed their noses at the king and, in an in-your-face gesture, the very first flag of the revolutionary forces bore for its emblem an image of a white pine. Not long after America gained its independence, the harvesting of pine began in earnest.

And why not? There were houses, schools, churches and stores to be built. The wood of the white pine was ideal for construction: creamy-white, light, even-grained, easy to work with and it took paint well. Fortune after fortune was made in the forests and intense lobbying in the halls of Congress assured that any talk of conservation would be held off until the trees were gone.

Michigan, of course, was no exception to this juggernaut of exploitation. More than a million acres of old-growth pine was felled, producing more money than all the gold found in California and building (according to those given to such numerical exercises) ten million six-room homes. There was an extraordinary amount of activity in the Upper Peninsula forests in the late nineteenth century and the first part of the twentieth century. The rivers—Escanaba, Manistique, Indian, Tahquamenon, to name a few—were clogged with pine logs. The sawmills were screaming day and night.

In my personal, non-dendrological lexicon, the white pine is patrician, dignified, and literally soars above all the crass commercialism swirling beneath its graceful boughs. White pines are indeed tall: in the old days they soared as high as 125, or even up to 170 feet tall. In the dense colonies where they thrived, the trunks grew straight and there were no branches for fifty feet or more. Its bark is dark gray and deeply furrowed. The soft, lustrous and aromatic needles grow in clusters of five and have a lacy appearance. The white pine cone is long, as much as five to eight inches, narrow and favored by red squirrels.

Those are the salient features of this magnificent tree. But what is it? No one knows, but what we *call* it is white pine. Perhaps there is too much analysis, cataloguing, managing, if you will. Maybe it is better to simply admire the white pine, to sit and listen to the wind making music in its boughs, to breathe in deeply of its redolence as it warms up on a summer day, to sink ourselves into the thick carpet of duff around its sturdy trunk.

Sadly, there are only a few small remnants of the old-growth white pine still blowing in the wind—the Estivant tract near the tip of the Keweenaw Peninsula, some virgin growth in the Porcupine Mountains in the far west of the Upper Peninsula and here and there, small outposts clinging on ridges and other remote places that loggers deemed too difficult to reach. One such spot is Laughing Whitefish Falls scenic site just a few miles east of our home.

It is usually spring when I go to meet with the elders, as I refer to this small grove of old-growth white pine. There is a particular spot where a triad of truly huge trees grows, three giants that tower over a hundred feet and exceed five feet in diameter through the trunk. Quietly, I sit on the thick carpet of fallen pine needles and contemplate these wondrous survivors of the lumbering frenzy. If I am lucky, a winter wren will give an impromptu concert and sing his tinkling refrain again and again. And I wonder why we had to cut so many of these majestic trees, and why so rapidly?

Well, it is easy for me to criticize, to ask hard questions from the vantage point of current knowledge and formal harvesting guidelines for lumbering companies. And I suppose it is easy to discern where my deepest affection lies among the three native pines. Jack, red and white pine, all abide in the Superior Peninsula. But the greatest of these is the white pine, for without this signature tree, the north country would lose much of its identity. To my way of thinking, the white pine is just as much a part of our heritage as music, cathedrals and art galleries.

SIX

Don't expect a light breakfast if you order a cinnamon roll at the Hilltop Restaurant. The Hilltop, a legend for good food for almost a half-century, is indeed located on the top of a hill overlooking the village of L'Anse. Before I renew my acquaintance with the attractive little resort town, I must stop as I always do at the Hilltop.

The Hilltop Restaurant is justly famous for its loaf-sized sweet roll. The staff gets a big kick out of serving the giant rolls to unsuspecting tourists and then watching their reactions to a cinnamon bun which literally fills a dinner plate. They offer no instructional manual for how to eat the huge treat. As usual, the restaurant is busy and as I wait for a server to take my order, I remember the day when a graduate student from India had a memorable encounter with a Hilltop roll.

I never learned why Ramesh chose to earn his Masters' degree in the far north at Northern Michigan University. But he was an excellent student and a good sport. Determined to sample an American lifestyle, at least as exemplified in the upper Midwest, he entered each new experience with unreserved enthusiasm. Ramesh was a talented observer, but his messages to his wife back home in Calcutta at first confused and then mildly alarmed her.

First, Ramesh started including weather reports in all his missives home. Her bewildered response: "Why are you telling me about the weather all the time?" Now weather is a salient, if not ubiquitous, topic of discussion in these environs. In India, Ramesh told us, there are just two seasons: the hot season and the monsoon. No one talked much about the weather in India.

Runjan was slightly more concerned when we took her husband to an ice-skating party and, the following weekend, for a snowshoe trek in the forest. Ramesh sent the faculty and his fellow students into gales of laughter when he told us what he had written to his confused wife (to whom ice and snow were completely foreign concepts). "First, I put on shoes with knives on the bottom and went sliding across a big floor of frozen water. Then they took me for a walk in the woods. I had to strap on huge web feet, like tennis racquets, and we all walked on top of snow!" But it is Ramesh's encounter with an immense sweet roll that I remember most vividly.

On our way north to Houghton to conduct a clinic for stutterers, the graduate students and I made the obligatory stop at the Hilltop. Ramesh told the waitress that he just wanted a breakfast roll and some hot tea. When the large cinnamon bun was set down before him, he muttered some expression of amazement in Hindi and then stared unbelievingly at the roll for thirty seconds while his fellow graduate students and the jokester professor watched in silent mirth. Then, grimly, and without saying a word throughout the entire meal, Ramesh attacked the giant roll. It took him quite a while but he finished it. For the rest of the day, Ramesh and the other students evaluated at least a dozen school-age children with stuttering problems and, all the while, that huge bolus of yeast dough worked its way painfully through his five-foot, four-inch, 120-pound body. He never told us what he wrote to his wife, Runjan, about this memorable gastrointestinal event.

Today, however, I hunger for a treat of a different type and when the server finally appears at my table, I order a wedge of the Hilltop's equally famous raspberry pie. Life is uncertain—I never pass up an opportunity for dessert. As always, the pie is outstanding. Just as I am nicely tucked into the delicious pastry, I notice an attractive blond woman striding purposefully toward my table. Her face is familiar and I rise to greet her. Wrapping me in a warm embrace, she gushes, "Dr. Emerick! It's so good to see you!" Noticing my hesitancy, she continues, "I'm Lori, Lori Lento—remember me? I'm Lori Quinn now. I work for the Copper Country Health Services. How long has it been, twenty years?"

Yes! I remember in a flash. Lori Lehto had been one of the brightest students I had known. Certainly she was the best therapist I had ever supervised. Lori was also an excellent athlete and had starred on the University's volleyball team during her undergraduate years. We had also shared an interest in Lewis and Clark's epic journey and, at the end of her therapy plans, she often wrote, "We proceeded on."

Lori sits down at my table and notices the unfinished slice of pie. "Still raspberry after all these years," she says. "I"m glad some things never change." We chat briefly—Lori is on her lunch break and has only a few minutes—and she tells me that her husband is a conservation officer with the Michigan Department of Natural Resources and that they have two daughters, Amy, twelve, and Cassie, seven. Life is good, she says. When she gets up to leave, Lori pauses and then says, "Thanks for being there and believing in me." Her tone is wistful and heartfelt. I notice that she has tears in her eyes. Giving me a long hug, she kisses me on the cheek and turns to leave.

By this time several other patrons, most notably men, are casting surreptitious glances at this balding, sixty-something male. After all, Lori is the image of Heather Locklear and today is stunning in a form-fitting red dress. As she strides toward the exit, all the male eyes in the room are riveted on the rewarding view. At a nearby table, a middle-aged man leans across the table and tells his companion, "I think I'll have what that old guy is having!"

I sit and muse a bit about my long, immensely satisfying tenure in the company of women. During a thirty-year teaching career in speech pathology, where more than 90% of the students are female, I was first a brother, then a father and finally—time to retire—a grandfather surrogate for scores of young women. What a blessing it has been! Even after fifteen years of retirement, many of these former students keep in touch and treat me like a member of their family. The attentiveness of these "adopted" daughters and granddaughters amuses many of my male friends.

One time, not too long ago, the members of the Thoreau Sauntering Club were enjoying post-hike refreshments in a Marquette cafe. The Sauntering Club is a group of five retired gents, all of us about the same age, who get together once a month for a walk in the woods. Usually we stop for coffee, scones or some other treat to extend and savor our outings.

On this particular occasion, we were enjoying a slab of cheesecake (raspberry, of course) when in rapid succession two of my surrogate daughters came up to the table and embraced me lovingly. I knew what was going to happen.

When I sat back down with the guys, the adolescent male bantering commenced, as I expected. Looking dramatically grave and doubtful, John said, "Yeah, sure, his *daughters*." Frank, our most vocal saunterer, and the one most likely to turn a situation into a salacious event, remarked something about Emerick and his harem. Having experienced this good-natured ribbing about my relationship with young women many times before, I decided to simply go with the flow.

"It happens all the time, guys," I said, putting on my best rueful expression, "Women just can't seem to leave me alone. In airports, restaurants and malls, beautiful gals come up and give me hugs. It's just a burden I've learned to endure."

The village of L'Anse is situated on a beautiful cove at the south end of vast Keweenaw Bay. The Chippewas who lived here for many years called the cove, *Wikwendong*, which means "bay." When Father Rene Menard coasted along this shore in search of souls in 1660, he renamed it *Bay L'Anse de Saint Therese*. As many old timers still do, my grandfather pronounced it "Lay-Anse."

When the first European explorers came to this area, they were after furs. Peter Crebessa, a former agent with the American Fur Company, came to L'Anse in 1838 and established a post to trade with the Chippewa. It was not long before clergymen followed the fur traders and established missions to the Indians. One of the first divines to build a church here, John H. Pitizel, established a Methodist mission in 1843. The Reverend Pitizel not only sought to convert the Chippewa, he also traveled long distances north to serve the Cornish miners at the newly-opened copper mines of Cliff and other locations. Not far away, up on the west shore of the bay, another clergyman, later to become famous as the Snowshoe Priest, established a Catholic mission. We will meet Frederic Baraga a bit further up the road.

In more modern times, a brief period of mining, a longer exportation of slate deposits, and then extensive lumbering provided an economic base for the community. There is still some logging going on and a fiber board company is located in L'Anse. The area is also a prime destination for visitors seeking recreational opportunities, something that an astute observer foresaw in 1911 when he predicted that L'Anse will become ". . . an ideal summer resort for those who really crave either rest or recreation."

When I drive down to the Bay, park the Silver Shrike by the shoreline and admire the ring-billed gulls wheeling over the water, I agree that this is indeed an ideal setting. Some recreational boaters might not have concurred in the mid-1960s when a seiche inundated the shore. Periodic movements of large lakes within their basins do occur, but usually the ebb and swell of a few inches is barely noticed. Everyone noticed the 5 1/2 foot surge in L'Anse, however, as it took out several sturdy docks and left many boats high and dry.

You can tell a lot about the character of local inhabitants and what they value by what they do with their most precious natural endowment, the lakeshore. I take a short stroll on the village shoreline and am impressed: there is an attractive public park with a marina, boat launch, benches, picnic tables, a walking path and a large new bandshell. A nearby poster lists the scheduled summer performances and I note that *White Water*, the Premo family band from Amasa, gave a concert here in early August. Dean Premo had encouraged me to talk with Steve and Roy Koski when I went through L'Anse on my pilgrimage and, glancing at my watch, I see that I must hurry over to Indian Country Sports to meet them.

A fact for the trivia contest: Indian Country Sports, located across from the marina and waterfront park, is the only sporting goods business in the United States that is also a working lighthouse. Let me go even further out on a yardarm and make this grandiose claim: it is the only sporting goods store in the entire world that is also a lighthouse. A working lighthouse. The United States Coast Guard certified the Indian Country Sports Light in 1998.

I must confess that I knew nothing about the uniqueness of Steve Koski's store when I met with him, his father, Roy, and his mother, Eila. People in the Superior Peninsula are invariably friendly and welcoming and the Koskis are no exception. Almost instantly I feel I am among friends and they field my questions without hesitation or suspicion.

Roy tells me that the Koski forebears came to this region in the 1920s, as did so many people of Finnish heritage, to eke out a living by farming, working in the woods and commercial fishing. The settlers liked the simple outdoor life here and put down roots.

"It's a great place to raise kids," Steve says. Roy and Eila nod in agreement.

"There is a sense of community here," Roy adds. In my travels in the U.P., I heard these comments again and again.

"How have things changed over the years?" I ask. Without a pause, both Steve and Roy respond that wealthy people from outside the area are buying up land, often at inflated prices that raise the local property taxes. The first thing some newcomers do is put up "No trespassing" signs, blocking the access of longtime residents to hunting and fishing spots that they have used for generations. Then, once the newcomers discover that the wide variety of supplies and services they are accustomed to in more populated areas is not available locally, they clamor for changes. These complaints are heard more frequently throughout the Upper Peninsula. Times they are a-changing and many of us who chose to live here long ago find the values of a simpler life we sought in this isolated region are under siege.

While Steve attends to his customers, I wander around the store with Roy. With the exception of bookstores and bakeries, the only kind of business in which I like to browse is a sporting goods store. I look at hunting bows and backpacks, fishing flies and flotation devices. I love it. Roy then asks casually if I would like to go up into the lighthouse tower. I look at him in astonishment, wondering if he is putting me on.

"No, really," Roy says, "See that metal spiral ladder? Let's go up and I'll show you around."

Mounting the ladder, I find myself stepping onto a narrow platform in the light chamber. A gull flies past and its raucous laugh seems a response to my incredulous stare.

"The tower is forty-four feet high," says Roy, "and it has the classic octagonal shape."

"This is fantastic!" I reply, gazing out at the sweeping view of Keweenaw Bay. When I express my amazement at the workmanship, Roy thanks me and then, softly, almost self-effacingly, he tells me that he built it.

In my dictionary of the regional lexicon, after the Finnish word, *SISU*, it says, "See Roy Koski." Patience. Courage. Endurance. It seems that Roy Koski built this amazing structure in part to prove the physicians at Mayo Clinic wrong in their dire predictions about his future. Following extensive surgery for a shoulder injury, Roy was told he would never again be able to use his arm for his beloved carpentry work. What did he do? Sit at home and lament his fate? No, Mr. Roy Koski got out his tools and undertook a major construction job: building a lighthouse tower on his son's store.

"And you know what?" he says with a twinkle in his eyes, "The shoulder works good." *SISU*!

As I leave, Roy asks me where my journey will take me next and I mention that I plan to make a brief trek up to Pequaming and Aura, both locations just a few miles north of L'Anse.

"Be sure to stop and see Wesley Ollila," Roy advises. Again I notice that twinkle.

The drive up the east side of Keweenaw Bay to Pequaming is a familiar excursion for me. When I was in my competitive running period, the Upper Peninsula Road Runners Club held an annual race along this scenic shore. There are also fond memories of times spent in the ghost town with our daughters.

Lynn and Mary loved going to Pequaming because they could create spontaneous one-act plays in a genuine old-time setting. When we first went there in 1968, much of the original village remained intact but eerily empty. The streets were wide and the entire area was shaded by large red oak trees. At least twenty of the cedar-shingled houses were still standing, as was the weathered clapboard Odd Fellows Hall. Except for the boarded-up windows, it was so tidy it seemed as if the towns-people were temporarily gone on some collective errand. We were so intrigued that we had to learn more about Pequaming.

Long ago, though a relatively short time in geological history, a narrow peninsula of sand and gravel jutted out into Keweenaw Bay. Gradually, the sand bar grew into a tombolo and "captured" an island just offshore. Shaped like a large mushroom, this idyllic spot has a long history of human habitation.

There is evidence that native peoples visited the area long before recorded history. Pointing to what seem to be remnants of stone cairns, some historians suggest that Vikings or perhaps even Celtic explorers from Wales or Ireland visited here many centuries before Columbus happened upon the West Indies.

The Chippewa called the almost-island *Pe-qua-qua-wa-ming* and considered it to be a sacred site. They camped here and held annual gatherings each summer. Fur traders and then the "Black Robes" paddled along the shores in search of beaver pelts and converts to Catholicism.

Charles Hebard, a land and timber speculator from Connecticut, appeared in the L'Anse area in 1877. Hebard saw the fine natural harbor at Pequaming and the vast stands of timber in the region. He built a large sawmill and commenced to produce lumber and shingles. But Mr. Hebard had a larger vision: as an immigrant from the British Isles, nostalgic about his homeland, he set out to build an English-style village with all the then-available amenities for his 240 workers and their families. By all accounts, the speculator from Connecticut was a benign and forward-looking owner, and life in Pequaming was probably as good as it got in the late nineteenth century rural America.

Pequaming townsite, 1964

By 1920, however, when the large tracts of merchantable timber were pretty much exhausted, along came Henry Ford in a black Model T. He saw that enough trees still remained to use in building wood panels for his cars. Ford liked Pequaming so much, he bought the entire village, including, as one cynic put it, all the people in it. Ever the paternalistic curmudgeon, Old Henry paid good wages, but in return he expected things to be run according to his exacting standards: the workers were expected to save some of their wages, take care of their homes, abstain from alcohol, cut their lawns, plant a garden (but keep no livestock) and drive only Ford automobiles—any color they wished as long as it was black.

The villagers very soon took Ford's measure. I would wager there were transplanted Yooper moles working in Henry's assembly plants who, upon hearing that Mr. Ford was intending to make a soiree to Pequaming, phoned a relative in the village and told them to get out the paint and brushes and tidy up. Henry liked tidy. One old-timer who had worked at the mill in Pequaming told me that Mr. Ford once snapped at his local supervisor: "Why does it always smell like paint when I come here? I thought you people were supposed to be sawing wood."

Slowly over the next two decades the lights of Pequaming flickered and then went out. The last high school class of nineteen students graduated in 1942. The almost-island subsequently passed through several owners and is platted now as ten-acre "Pequaming Shore Parcels." The only remnants of a bustling era are the hulk of the old sawmill, a water tower with the familiar Ford logo, and the former Ford bungalow which is rented out to summer tourists.

As the village of Pequaming was slowly dying, a number of workers of Finnish descent moved their families four miles to the east and founded a small farming community. Charles Hebard tried to make the transition easier by offering land at bargain rates. Tobias Hiltunen is thought to be the first settler; after the devastating labor problems in the Keweenaw Copper mines, many others followed. They named the new community *Aura*, which is the Finnish word for "plow."

Although not rich farming country, the settlers found that the clay loam produced good crops of potatoes and grain. A milk cow, a pig or two, some chickens and plenty of *SISU* and they got by. "It sure beat going down in the mine," said Wesley Ollila.

When I arrive at the Ollila homestead in Aura, Mrs. Ollila is busy making pasties. As a Cousin Jack raised on traditional Cornish pasties, I observe the mound of shredded carrots she is adding to the meat and potatoes and involuntarily wince. A rare spasm of tact keeps me from commenting and I keep my Celtic mouth shut, at least until it's time to eat the pasties.

Wesley was a maker of extraordinary wooden sleighs—he had to give up the work because of health reasons—and still a master story teller. He is justly proud of helping initiate the annual Aura Music Jamboree. Each July hundreds of people come to Aura to hear folk, country and traditional Finnish music. Since the park grounds and township hall where the festival occurs are right next door to the Ollila home, Wesley helps out at the event any way he can. Between infectious chuckles, he tells me a story about a refined lady visitor and the traditional offering of bean soup:

> *Every year we make a really big batch of bean soup for the guests—we use a fifty-five-gallon drum. To stir the soup, we use a canoe paddle. So, this one lady, really dressed up she was and a bit snooty, you know, came up and watched our operation for a while. Seems like she couldn't decide whether to take a chance and buy a bowl of soup or not. She asked a bunch of questions. Finally, someone gave her a little cup of the soup to taste and she keeps poking around in it with a spoon. Well, she took a sip or two, and right then, I decide to have some fun. So, I say to my buddy kinda loud like, 'Hey, I know what happened to that chipmunk that was*

around here begging for food—he's in the soup!' Now that old gal, she spit
out a mouthful of bean soup, dropped the cup and hightailed it outta here!

As long as I am this close to Skanee, another small town north of L'Anse, I thought I might try to find the remains of a single-room log cabin where James Oliver Curwood wrote his autobiography, *Son of the Forest* in the winter of 1922. I learn that the cabin was located fifteen miles northeast of Skanee. One local resident tells me that the old log structure was moved to a park north of L'Anse. But the urgency is on me, to say nothing of the Silver Shrike, to get back on U.S. Highway 41 and continue the quest.

So I turn south toward L'Anse. I won't even think of trying to find Mt. Arvon which, at 1,979.238 feet is the highest geographical point in Michigan. The directions to Mt. Arvon in the Baraga County Tourism and Recreation Association brochure leave me reeling. I quote a small portion of the text:

> *The route on Ravine Road is as follows: At 0.7 miles, fork, go straight; 1.8 miles pass through gravel pit; 2.0 miles, leave gravel pit at a fork, go straight; 3.0 miles, fork, bear left; 3.4 miles, fork, bear right . . .*

And there are three more inches of single-spaced "directions!" Then, in a wonderfully-worded caveat, the reader is informed that "due to logging operations, the roads are often changed." And that, for those still undaunted and mindless explorers, "the roads are impossibly muddy in spring and clogged with snow in winter."

Some folks make a quest of finding and climbing the highest point in every state. Perhaps I'm being a spoilsport here, but let's put this highest point obsession in perspective. Consider: Lake Superior is six hundred feet above sea level and Mt. Arvon is just shy of two thousand feet—that gives you some idea of what we call "mountains" in Michigan. Besides—and now my crotchety Luddite persona re-emerges—the waste rock pile from open pit iron mining operations southeast of Negaunee is now actually the highest point in Michigan and climbing even as we watch. I find that Chambers of Commerce frown upon such revelations, so in the spirit of free inquiry I consider it my duty to pass it along.

As U.S. 41 swings north from L'Anse, it ascends a rocky hill and offers a very pleasant, sweeping vista of Keweenaw Bay. This side of the Bay is Baraga Country:

I am in Baraga County; the Bishop Baraga Shrine is on my left; soon I will pass Baraga State Park; and, in a few miles, I will be in the village of Baraga. Who was this cleric and how did he come to be known as the Shepherd of the Wilderness?

Frederic Baraga was born in Slovenia in 1797 to a family of great wealth. Orphaned in his teens, he first studied law in Vienna and then answered a call to holy orders. A well-educated young priest and an accomplished linguist, Baraga sought and was given a mission to Native Americans living around the Great Lakes. After serving near Traverse City, on Beaver Island and at LaPointe, Wisconsin, Father Baraga came to the L'Anse area in 1843 to establish a mission among the Chippewa. In today's social climate, his stated goal of "eradicating ignorance and vice among the Indians" would be very politically incorrect, but in the context of the times, the mission was openly advocated. Father Baraga named his mission site *Assinins* after a local native chief who became his first convert.

Baraga, apparently a man of great energy and zeal, helped the Indians build cabins close to his log chapel, devised grammar and prayer books in the Chippewa language, sought to eliminate the local practice of exchanging liquor for furs, and still found time to trek all about the Keweenaw Peninsula ministering to copper miners and their families. His travels on snowshoes are legendary. One winter Father Baraga walked from L'Anse to Copper Harbor, a distance of sixty miles, in four days; he spent three nights wrapped in a blanket with only a small fire for warmth. Perhaps it was on this trek the good father allowed himself to grumble in his journal that ". . . this is a sad, sterile and unpleasant place to live."

In 1853, Baraga, by then known widely as the Snowshoe Priest, was consecrated as a bishop and left his mission at Assinins to live first in Sault Ste. Marie and then, after 1866, in Marquette.

The Shepherd of the Wilderness by all accounts was a very humble, devout and temperate person. He chose to give away his clothing and other possessions to those in need. When Bishop Baraga moved to Marquette to establish his diocese in the city, the local residents wanted to honor him with a public reception but he would not permit it. Baraga died in 1868 and the Catholic Church is in the process of considering his canonization. I'm not sure that the humble Snowshoe Priest would have permitted himself to be made a saint, either.

So now, let me ask you: what would the ascetic, unassuming Baraga think about a shrine overlooking Keweenaw Bay which features a thirty-five foot tall gilded statue of himself holding a seven-foot cross and wearing snowshoes twenty-six feet long?

Full of self-righteousness and smug certainty that I *know* what Father Baraga's response to the shrine would be, I proceed on to the village named for the

Shepherd of the Wilderness. Baraga is the home of Pettibone, a manufacturing company that makes large, innovative machines used in logging. Even a tree-hugger like me is impressed when seeing what these machines can do in the woods. The small town is also the site of a large casino and a relatively new maximum security prison, one of several penal institutions built in the Upper Peninsula during the past decade or so.

I want to see what some of the local residents have to say about the new prison in their backyard. Stopping at a convenience store to fill up the Silver Shrike's gullet and get a soft drink, it is soon apparent that the townspeople do not want to talk about the correctional facility. At least they don't want to talk about it to an outsider arriving one autumn day in a silver pickup. I get shrugs and short responses like, "It's good for the economy," and "It provides jobs."

"Any downside to the prison being here?" I ask a painfully thin man filling up his rusty old Chevrolet.

"Like what?" he counters, his eyes riveted on the pump.

"Well, like when relatives of the inmates move here to be close—could that create any problems?"

"Don't know nothin' about that," he replies in a tone that clearly indicates the end of the conversation.

The powers-that-be who plan where to build prisons are shrewd. They always look for the path of least political resistance. Governments wanting to build prisons target a region that is isolated, has a small number of residents and, perhaps most important of all, is economically depressed. It is the same for agencies seeking a location for a toxic waste site. They make many promises of future jobs, spend a lot of money on construction, and appeal to the economic aspirations of local merchants. It is a canny strategy. The community becomes a repository for some of the most toxic elements of society and the planners know that there will be few, if any, objections from the local residents.

Once again my fair Muse is annoyed at me for bringing up an unpleasant topic in such a beautiful place, so I tap rhythmically on the steering wheel and hum a few bars of *Greensleeves*. I promise her that soon we will pass a spot that reflects the promise, endurance and indomitable nature of the human spirit. But before that, we will encounter the first evidence that we are indeed about to enter the Copper Country.

It takes a few minutes for the neophyte sojourner to realize that the sand beaches of Keweenaw Bay north of Baraga are dark gray, almost black. When you stop—the highway hugs the shoreline here—and pick up some of the sand, you find that it has a gritty, almost metallic texture, and that it leaves a dark powdery residue on your hands. This "stamp sand" is waste from the copper mines. In the process of extracting copper from its rocky carapace, the ore was crushed in large, noisy

Lon Emerick

Indian Country Sports Shop Lighthouse, L'Anse

The Hanka Farm, Askel Hill

stamp mills; one of them, the Mass Mill, was located near here. After the copper was siphoned off, the sandy waste was dumped in the Bay. Since the Keweenaw Bay is an arm of Lake Superior, the counterclockwise current washed this dark residue up on the shore.

The dreams, courage and endurance of our ancestors are alive and well in the Superior Peninsula. From this heritage of self-reliance and persistence in the face of adversity, we derive our fierce sense of independence and, yes, too, our irritability when well-meaning but misguided outsiders come north to offer us enlightenment. The saga of Askel Hill and the Hanka Farm reveals that those who came before us actually lived the truism: *One must be long in a place to belong*.

In 1890, five Finnish woodsmen, Peter Tauriainen, John Sotaneimi, Andrew Heikkinen, Joseph Karky and Enoch Pyykkonen found a hill near Otter Lake. Three miles inland from Lake Superior, Askel Hill, as it was later to be named, had been an island in the bay of an ancient lake, the precursor of Lake Superior. On this six mile long, two mile wide hill, the woodsmen acquired land under the Homestead Act. Other Finnish immigrants decided to settle there as well.

The Hanka family, Herman and Lena and their four grown children, came to the area to homestead in 1896. Herman Hanka had survived a blasting accident in a Calumet copper mine but sustained injuries that rendered him deaf and altered his personality. Herman was over fifty years old when he came to Askel Hill, so his children did most of the labor as the family cleared eighteen acres, built the house, barn, an obligatory sauna and several other outbuildings. The younger Hankas also hunted for wild game, repaired machinery for other homesteaders and worked in the woods in the winter. One son, apparently the most enterprising of the children, Johan Nikolai, known as Nik, gave Askel Hill its name. In Finnish, Askel means "step." Nik thought it would be an apt name for the community because of the poor corduroy road. Logs were laid crosswise on the road bed leading to the hill; in order to negotiate the road, the walker had to constantly watch his step so as not to get mired between the logs.

When Nik died in the 1920s, so did the driving force for change on the Hanka Farm. Although his easy-going brother Jallu lived at the homestead until 1966, he left the farm pretty much as it had been when Nik passed away forty years before. The Hanka farm was frozen in time, a relic of the Finnish pioneer self-sufficient lifestyle. The old farm has been restored as a museum and is now part of the newly-minted Keweenaw National Historical Park.

SEVEN

Follow your passion, the sage advises. Seek that which you love to do, make it your life's mission and surely you will know peace and harmony of spirit. Let me offer a caveat: you will not find your calling by an obsessive inward pursuit. The answers to life's questions are not found in the navel. In his monumental book, *Blue Highways*, Least Heat Moon writes that the greatest of the Grandfathers' vision is this:

"To seek a higher concord, man looks not deeper within—he reaches farther out."

A former teacher once said that a *job* is what someone else wants done and pays you for doing it. *Work* is something you would embrace willingly even if you didn't get paid. Many are called by their passions, but only a few can or will choose to follow.

Mark Silver has found his passion: he is the maker of exquisitely crafted firearms. No, not just a fabricator of guns, he is a creator of period flintlock rifles. While some may question how instruments of possible violence can be described this way, in my view Mark's rifles are extraordinary works of art. His creations also keep alive the craftsmanship of prior generations and link the present in a tangible way with the past.

Mark and his wife Mary Hindelang live in a remote area southwest of Chassel. Their home is poised on a high bank overlooking the Pike River—it reminds me so much of my Foster Greek Homestead that I feel an immediate sense of calm and comfort as I approach the front door. Emerging from the door of his walkout basement door of his workshop, Mark's greeting is just as warm as the setting.

A pleasant looking man of medium height with silver hair and an impressive moustache, Mark Silver's enthusiasm for his work spills out of him like water from an artesian well. Clearly, here is a person who is doing exactly what he was meant to do. A decade or so ago, he and Mary abandoned their positions as human services professionals in the city to pursue a simpler and richer life in the country. They have never looked back.

I ask Mark to show me how he proceeds with his craft. Turning to his workbench, he directs my attention to a firearm he had been working on when I arrived.

"This is a 1810, London .54 caliber sporting rifle," he says, taking the gun from a vise. "It's about two-thirds done." After spending considerable time with a customer—finding out his expectations and what he intends to do with the firearm—Mark prepares an elaborate plan.

First, the stock is carefully fashioned from a block of maple or other wood. The barrel is then meticulously fitted to the wood and the internal mechanisms—trigger, hammer, pan and frizzen (where the flint hits to create a spark)—are installed.

"The final tasks are checkering the stock and engraving the barrel and receiver," Mark concludes.

"How long does this take?" I ask, looking through some of his photographs depicting engravings of elaborate Celtic loops.

"The engraving takes several weeks," he says, "and it usually takes me a year or so to finish a rifle."

I whistle in amazement. Much has been gained by mass production and interchangeable parts. My Ithaca 20 gauge shotgun is identical to my neighbor's and, if we wished, we could exchange barrels or trigger mechanisms. But what has been lost by our efficient machinery? The flintlock rifles I see here in Mark Silver's workshop all reflect the individualized expression of pride, personal satisfaction and the spirit of their crafter.

"Let's go upstairs and you can meet Mary," Mark suggests after he puts away his tools. I almost demur, thinking about the miles I must go before I see my ancestors' home place. But I'm glad I decide to stay. Mary Hindelang is warm, gracious and has the demeanor of someone who expects something good is going to happen soon. A former nurse, she earned a Ph.D. in ecology and is conducting ongoing research with the moose population in Isle Royale National Park. Mary teaches ecology and environmental education at Michigan Technological University in Houghton. I like her very much.

Noticing that I am fidgeting, Mary asks, "Where do you go next on your pilgrimage?"

"I am off to Houghton to see what the Little Doctor wrought," I reply, as I rise to leave.

"Give our regards to wee Douglass," she says.

Returning to U.S. Highway 41, I resolve to offer my admiration to Dr. Douglass Houghton, the man who started the first great mineral stampede in North America.

Although couched in conservative language and containing explicit cautions to the naive, the Little Doctor's geological report still precipitated the first large land rush and mineral boom in the young United States of America. The guarded excitement in this sentence of Douglass Houghton's scholarly treatise caught the imagination of fortune seekers: "Upon the whole (while I would carefully avoid exciting any unfounded expectations among our citizens, and caution them to avoid engaging in wild schemes with a view to gain sudden wealth), the examinations and surveys which have been made would serve fully to justify the conclusion that this region of the country will prove a continued source of wealth to our State." That did it. In 1841, thousands of speculators, prospectors and adventure seekers (but, curiously, few if any experienced hard-rock miners) headed straight for the remote and wild Keweenaw Peninsula. It is fitting that an historic city in the Copper Country, now home of Michigan Technological University which started as a college of mining engineering, is named for Dr. Houghton.

Born in Troy, New York, the diminutive Douglass Houghton was a five-foot, four-inch man for all seasons: chemist, physician, geologist, educator, politician, wilderness explorer, accomplished flute player. Endowed with a keen inquiring mind and boundless energy, he joined Schoolcraft in discovering the source of the Mississippi River at Itasca, Minnesota, served as mayor of Detroit and helped organize the University of Michigan—all before his untimely death at the age of thirty-four! But it is for his geological surveys of the Upper Peninsula that he is best known. Commissioned the first State geologist in 1840, Houghton was allotted the sum of $3,000 and charged with conducting an analysis of the possible mineral wealth in the vast reaches of the Peninsula recently acquired by the State as a consolation prize in the mini-war with Ohio over the Toledo Strip. Accompanied by three assistants, Dr. Houghton systematically explored the region for mineral wealth.

In the Keweenaw Peninsula (Chippewa for "place of crossing"), a rocky finger of land which curves out into Lake Superior, Houghton found traces of copper almost everywhere he looked. Most of the metal he found was "float" copper, chunks of native copper which had been discarded capriciously by the glaciers which scoured the region thousands of years before. Native or "free" copper is not combined with sulphide or oxide; the Keweenaw Peninsula is the only place on the planet where large quantities exist. Douglass Houghton did not live to see later discoveries of the bonanza lodes of copper found in ancient laval flows (amygdaloid) and sedimentary beds of sand and gravel (conglomerate) which brought fleeting wealth and glory to the area.

On the evening of October 13, 1845, the young geologist was steering a Mackinaw boat on a course toward Eagle River when a wet snowstorm erupted on Lake Superior. A sudden gust capsized the boat, throwing the men in the icy waves. Only two men, Peter McFarland and Baptiste Bodrie, managed to reach shore and relate the tragic death of the Little Doctor who played such a big part in the development of the Copper Country.

Centuries before Douglass Houghton searched for mineral wealth, even long before the Chippewa tribes camped along the shores of the Keweenaw, a mysterious race of miners looking for copper hacked shallow pits, ten to twenty feet deep, into the flinty hills. Throughout the area, early prospectors found these ancient pits; most of the later prosperous copper mines were located on the ancient sites. The Chippewas did not know of the people who had mined in the region and did not use the metal themselves, although they revered it as a manifestation of the Great Spirit. Who were these prehistoric miners—Vikings, Phoenicians, Central American Indians? They left no remnants of dwellings, pottery, burial sites or personal artifacts, just hundreds of crude stone hammers, abandoned in the pits as if their users were ready to begin mining again tomorrow. Whoever they were, these early miners were prodigious workers: it is estimated that it would have required at least a thousand men working for a thousand years to remove the quantity of copper they extracted by the primitive methods employed. Their mining techniques, albeit crude, were effective. Fires built against copper-bearing rock and cold water poured over the hot rock caused the boulders to spall; the miners then hammered the copper free from chunks of the boulder. Carbon dating of the charcoal remains from their fires indicates that the mining commenced as early as five thousand years ago—then suddenly ceased about A.D. 1400. Archaeologists have traced weapons and other artifacts of Michigan copper all the way down to the Yucatan Peninsula in Mexico and in Central America.

In the mid-seventeenth century, Jesuit missionaries learned of the rich copper deposits during their travels along the south shore of Lake Superior. The Chippewas escorted Father Dablon up the Ontonagon River to show him an immense boulder of pure native copper lying free in the riverbed. Alexander Henry, sole English survivor of the 1763 massacre at Fort Michilimackinac, also visited the boulder; he made an abortive attempt at mining in the area in 1771. Schoolcraft and other explorers inspected the now-famous boulder, chipped off specimens of the copper and described it in their journals. But it took an enterprising American, James Eldred, to devise a scheme for making money from the slab of copper (unlike granite, the Ontonagon boulder is a slab, four feet, six inches long, four feet wide and only seventeen inches thick). He skidded the boulder out of the river and exhibited it in Detroit in the fall of 1843 with an admission fee of 25¢ per person. Although copper was obviously not a precious metal, and there were then very few uses for it (copper was not used for making brass for bullets until the Civil War, and electrical wiring was, of course, unheard-of) a flood of treasure seekers arrived the next summer at the very tip of the Keweenaw Peninsula.

Almost a hundred mining companies were formed and the hopeful seekers explored and dug but, in the end, only eight of the organizations paid dividends to their investors. The early prospectors did not know that the major deposits of copper lay in a narrow band, three to five miles wide and more than a hundred miles long, on an elevated greenstone ridge which cuts down the center of the Keweenaw Peninsula.

Houghton: population 7,498. A friend of mine says he dislikes even driving through this largest city on the Keweenaw Peninsula—the rows of old red brick buildings make him feel depressed. Not me. I love it. These vintage structures remind me of our pioneer roots, of the people who came to this remote and rugged land and made a place for those to follow. Besides, the modern "shopping troughs" have spread southwest of town on a different highway, so you can go through Houghton on U.S. 41 without seeing a Wal-Mart, Pizza Hut or Taco Bell, something I consider a small blessing.

When I traveled in the British Isles several years ago, I was impressed by the way the past is saved and treasured. Instead of tearing down an old building, as we do so readily in the United States, they lovingly repair and restore it. On the streets of London, and in many other cities and towns in England, I marveled at plaques on buildings declaring that Charles Dickens or Somerset Maugham had frequented a particular pub or that Emily Brönte's mother once lived in this stone cottage.

As far as I know, there is no plaque on any building in Houghton proclaiming that Ransom Shelden raised a glass of beer herein. Fittingly, however, the main business street is named for Shelden, the first entrepreneur to build a store serving the movers and shakers of the copper boom in 1852.

Ransom (what were his parents thinking?) left Wisconsin in 1846 with his wife and two children to seek his fortune in northern Michigan. The family sailed up Lake Michigan, through the Straits of Mackinac, portaged around the falls on the St. Marys River at the Soo and landed finally at Copper Harbor, a small village at the tip of the Keweenaw Peninsula. Shelden was flat broke but hopeful that there was a fortune to be made in the new mineral rush.

Shelden was right. Seeing that food was in short supply in the copper mining towns, he chartered a boat on speculation, sailed to L'Anse and loaded the hold with potatoes. After all his expenses were deducted, he cleared $300 from the sale of his cargo. Shelden parlayed this modest beginning into a fortune. According to the 1860 census, Ransom Shelden was worth $125,000, making him the wealthiest man in the Upper Peninsula. That may not seem like a lot of money by a twenty-first century standard, yet consider what food items cost in 1860: one pound of coffee, 16¢; a dozen eggs, 15¢; an 18 pound ham, $2.25.

As I drive through the bustling campus of Michigan Technological University, I

Mark Silver, master craftsman

Detail on a flintlock

Lift bridge over the Portage Canal, Houghton County

Old Reliable, Shaft 2

wonder what Ransom Shelden would think about this widely respected institution of higher education. I conclude he would approve. Starting in 1885 as the Michigan School of Mines, Tech now attracts students from all over the world to its rigorous science and engineering programs. MTU has very serious students, most of them male. When I taught at a sister institution, Northern Michigan University, some of my female students dated men from Michigan Tech. The young women told me later how startled they were to discover that their dates, waiting for them in the dormitory lobby, were using the time for studying!

When you cross over the famous lift bridge between Houghton and Hancock, you appreciate the ingenuity and dedication of the engineers who designed it. Maybe they too studied calculus and structural analysis while waiting for their dates.

The Portage Lake waterway cuts the Keweenaw Peninsula into south and north portions. At one time, this waterway provided a shortcut and safe passage for ships making the transit from Keweenaw Bay to western Lake Superior.

In the early days of the copper boom, travelers had to rely on a ferry to get them across the waterway from Houghton to Hancock. An irascible old English sailor by the name of Captain Samuel Esles took people across, usually only when he felt like it. I suspect he was a Cornishman.

The first bridge was built in 1876 and the enterprising investor charged tolls for passage: humans, 5¢; cattle and mules, 15¢; hogs, 10¢. The modern bridge with the middle span that lifts to allow larger boats to pass was built in 1959. Some statistics for those with an engineering bent: 1,310 feet long with a lift span of 260 feet; when the span section is hoisted, there is 104 feet of clearance for passing ships; the twin towers lifting the span are 180 feet tall. In a few flashes of his chrome hubcaps, the Silver Shrike carries me across this marvel of engineering to Hancock.

When he signed his name to the Declaration of Independence with a large and sweeping signature, John Hancock endeared himself to the people of our young nation. In addition to Michigan, there are seventeen other states with a town named after the patriot.

The town of Hancock (population 4,547) was platted by Samuel Worth Hill, acting as a representative of the Quincy Mining Company. Mr. Hill arrived on the Keweenaw Peninsula in 1845 as a member of a geological survey team. What he is remembered most for, though, is his legendary swearing. Apparently the man could really cuss, so much so that he stood out even among the many rough characters drifting about the Lake Superior country at the time. The expression, "What in the Sam Hill," became a socially acceptable alternative for, "What the hell." Everybody has some talent and Sam, by all accounts, was the leader of the pack when it came to expletives.

Hancock has a rich Finnish heritage. Right at this moment I pass Finlandia University, the only institution of higher education in the United States created by and for Finnish people. Founded in 1896 as Suomi College, Finlandia now attracts students of many ethnic heritages. They even have a book of mine, *The Superior Peninsula*, for sale in their campus bookstore—a self-important criterion I use for evaluating the quality of libraries and universities.

My anticipation quickens now as U.S. Highway 41 curves sharply to the north and heads steeply up Quincy Hill. The Silver Shrike relishes the new challenge, shifts down into a lower gear and leans into the hill. Soon, Shaft House Number 2, a remnant of Old Reliable, looms into view. I am entering the richest mineral lands of the region.

They called it Old Reliable because the Quincy Mine continued to produce copper and pay dividends for more than a half-century. Although three companies sank shafts on Quincy Hill, the Quincy mine outproduced the others; the successful owners then acquired the Pewabic and Franklin mines. They dug deeply into the hill. The Quincy mine shafts extend 9,260 feet under the waters of Portage Lake and into the very bowels of the earth. The ore mined here was amygdaloid (a Greek word for almond-shaped) copper, pure red metal found in the bubble cavities of igneous rock.

Several shafts were sunk to retrieve the rich lode and around each mining location a residential community for workers swiftly blossomed. Coburntown, Limerick, French Town, Hardscrabble were just a few of the communities. Those were the boom days and everyone thought it would never end; they thought the red metal would last forever and a day.

Shaft House Number 2 sits poised over a deep shaft and houses an immense hoist which lowered men into the depths and brought both workers and ore to the surface. It is silent now except during the summer season. Refurbished as a tourist attraction, Number 2 stands today as a much-photographed sentinel overlooking the towns of Hancock and Houghton.

EIGHT

Heading north from Quincy Hill I am now breathing the purest, most vitalizing air on earth. It says so right on the roadside sign. A bit of hyperbole offered by the tourist bureau, perhaps, but I am energized by the thought that soon I will be in Calumet, the very same town in which my mother was born, where my grandparents and great-grandparents lived and worked. I want to walk on the streets where they walked, see again the old company house that was their home and visit the coffee shop with vintage dark wood booths where they talked and dreamed of the future.

First, I must make a short diversion through Laurium and then to Lake Linden to call upon two other former residents of this historic region, one a famous college football player who died young, and the other my all-time favorite speech therapy patient.

Laurium: named by city fathers who apparently were antiquarians, after a mining town in Attica, a district of ancient Greece. Well away from the noise and dust of the copper mines in Calumet, Laurium was favored as a place to live by more wealthy residents of the booming area. I am going through the small town to visit the memorial for an athlete who is forever linked to the 40th president of the United States.

George Gipp was born on February 15, 1895, and died from complications of tonsillitis on December 14, 1920. An extraordinary football player at Notre Dame University, he became a legend in his own time. In a four-year career he scored 83 touchdowns in only 32 games. Well before the days of kicking tees, Gipp drop-kicked a *62-yard field goal!* It took a Hollywood film to extend and embellish the legend. The story is that, as he lay dying, George Gipp (played by Ronald Reagan) told his coach Knute Rockne (played by Pat O'Brien) that in some future game when Notre Dame was not faring well, he could motivate the players by asking them to "win one for the Gipper."

After pausing briefly at the Gipp Memorial, I move on to thoughts of another inspiring person who graced my life. During my time at the university, Dorothy Bonini had a motivating impact not unlike that of the Gipper on several generations of speech pathology students. Following a massive stroke, she came to our clinic with a severe language impairment; for a while the only word she could utter was "shit!"

We were amazed at the nuances of meaning she could convey with that single expletive. We were even more impressed by what a warm, open and sincere person Dorothy was; despite her own limitations and concerns, she took a familial interest in the young students. They in turn worked diligently in therapy sessions, took her on field trips to practice her shaky, newly-acquired communication skills and even visited at her Lake Linden home for follow-up treatment. At the end of a five-week intensive therapy program, Mrs. Bonini had improved dramatically. She radiated confidence in herself. She resumed using the telephone, clipped and studied advertisements in the local newspaper, began to shop for the family groceries without assistance and started the immense job of sorting and filing her large collection of ethnic recipes. She even acquired a pamphlet of traffic rules and began preparing to reacquire her driver's license, which had lapsed during her recovery from the stroke.

During the therapy process—we saw her intermittently for several years—I encouraged Dorothy to keep a diary of her thoughts, feelings and observations. The daily journal prompted her to undertake a new and encompassing challenge: to tell her own story of the brain injury, convalescence and eventual recovery.

It took her more than a year to edit the entries, interview relatives and piece together the fragments of her recollections. Several times she almost abandoned the task in frustration, but finally the booklet, which she titled *Comeback After A Stroke*, was completed. When the booklet was printed and she held it in her hands for the first time, Mrs. Bonini looked fondly at the members of her therapy team who had assembled for a reception in her honor and said, "You have given me back my life." There was not a dry eye in the room.

Although Dorothy Bonini is gone now, her optimism, energy and compassion live on in the lives and memories of a score of speech therapists who worked with her.

The most appropriate thing I could think of to do in Lake Linden was to stop at Lindell's Chocolate Shoppe, the last place I met and talked with Dorothy before she died. When I order only a cup of coffee and say I am communing with an old friend, the young server keeps a wary eye on me. Dorothy would have been as amused as I am—we shared a zany sense of humor and tendency to laugh in circumstances that others might consider embarrassing or even troublesome.

Dorothy would have also been amused by an incident that occurred a few years ago at the nearby hamlet of Gay. Named for himself by Joseph E. Gay, the town was the site of two copper smelting mills, the Mohawk and the Wolverine. During the copper mining heyday in the early 1900s, more than 1,500 people lived here. Now the former town is pretty much abandoned.

But there is a Gay Bar. What I mean to say is, there is a bar in Gay and it is called *The Gay Bar*. The character of this saloon is decidedly macho. At one time, the owner was a weapons collector; bayonets, swords and more than 240 guns were displayed on the walls and hanging from the ceiling.

One warm spring day in May, a friend and I were engaged in a marathon birding challenge; the object was to see as many species as possible in a specified time, in this case a twenty-four-hour period. When we tumbled into the Gay Bar at noon that day, we had been up since before dawn trolling first for owls near the rental cabin, then birds of prey on Brockway Mountain Drive, and finally shorebirds along Lake Superior by Bete Grise. We were giddy with success—we already had eighty-nine different species of birds recorded and the entire afternoon and evening to expand our list.

We didn't smell trouble right away. We smelled. Very sweetly. In order to endure the waves of mosquitoes and blackflies, we had drenched ourselves in Avon Skin-So-Soft and now the local good old boys in the bar were picking up the waves of perfume emanating from the two animated bird-watchers.

Some adult males still regard birdwatching as an effete, maybe even feminine, pursuit and soon Jim and I were on the receiving end of long, suspicious stares. Then the muttering began. We could almost hear them saying: "What are *they* doing in here? Have them *boys* lost their way? What kind of a bar do *they* think this is anyway?"

As I make my way back to Calumet I laugh aloud and honk the horn, remembering the aromatic adventure in Gay. My Britannic Muse smiles and claps her wee hands. We are going to visit the site of the richest copper strike on the Keweenaw Peninsula.

The glory years of the Copper Country really began with the discovery of the *great* Calumet and Hecla conglomerate deposits (a form of ore where pure copper fills the open spaces around deposits of sand and pebbles) near the present communities of Calumet and Laurium. It earned the adjective great in every way; at one time the Calumet and Hecla Company employed 66,000 people, and between 1869 and 1946 paid over two hundred million dollars in dividends for the investors. The company sank twenty-one shafts to depths from four to six thousand feet; during the era of peak production, more than fifty miles of tunnels were dug under the mining locations of Red Jacket, Blue Jacket, Yellow Jacket, Albion and others. All these mining locations were known collectively as Calumet.

According to a local anecdote, the rich deposit was found on September 17, 1864, by Billy Royall, an Irish saloon and hotel keeper, who was looking for his lost pigs. He heard squealing from between the roots of a tree and when he pulled out one of his pigs, a chunk of copper came along with the creature. More probably it

Fifth street in Calumet, late 1800s

was Edwin J. Hulbert, civil engineer and nephew of Henry Rowe Schoolcraft, who found outcroppings of ore while surveying for a road between Hancock and Eagle River. Later, after a dispute over management, Alexander Agassiz, son of the Swiss naturalist Louis Agassiz, took over direction of the Calumet and Hecla Company. *Calumet* is French for "pipe of peace," while *Hecla* was the name of a volcano in Iceland.

The Calumet and Hecla flourished in the late 1800s, and the population of the area reached 100,000 persons (now down to 30,000). It was a veritable melting pot of nationalities—Cornish, Finnish, French Canadians, Italians, Irish and many others. Long before it became a trendy politically-correct objective, the bustling mining community in the wilds of northern Michigan featured astounding ethnic diversity.

During those glory years C&H was the major producer of copper in the United States, and some of the residents could apparently afford their desires for culture in the isolated north country. There was much local pride when a large ornate opera house was erected in Calumet; at the time it was the only theatre owned by a municipality in the United States. Designed by C.K. Shand, a Detroit architect, it featured a proscenium arch 66 feet wide and 60 feet high; the stage is 28 feet deep. The

Calumet Opera House was completed on March 20, 1900, for the then-extravagant cost of $59,815.18. Lillian Russell, John Philip Sousa and Jane Addams appeared on the stage before sellout crowds. The Calumet Theatre has been refurbished in recent years. It remains a lovely building—at least seventy-five events are held here every year.

By 1910, the mines were wearing out and the copper boom days were almost over; shafts descended far into the earth and it was becoming very expensive to bring ore to the surface. What was it like for the men who toiled in the mines during the boom years and how did it all come unraveled so swiftly? The Satterlys, Trezonas and Harrises know because they lived it, and now I have come here to honor their labors and legends. But there is something I must do first to fulfill a family tradition: I must get a Cornish pasty to sustain my body and soul.

In my mother's family, there was no clear line between religion and the making of pasties. Every Sunday morning after church, my mother, her sister and my grandmother would assemble the ingredients: meat, usually beef round steak, cut into bite-sized chunks; potatoes (always soaked in water ahead of time) cut into small pieces; chopped onion; and, a final dollop, a pat of butter atop the mound. And then the crust was wrapped around the ingredients. Oh, the crust! It was always divinely flaky. The initials of each family member gathered for the weekly feast were inscribed on a crescent-shaped pasty. The ladies always made a couple of extra Cornish delights for unexpected guests.

It was difficult to pin the cooks down about a precise recipe for a pasty, or for almost any creation for that matter; it was always a pinch of this, a dash of that. And they worked so fast that it was hard to follow exactly what they did. But they were rigorous about the baking of pasties.

"Start them at 400 degrees," Grandmother Harris insisted, "and, after fifteen minutes, turn down the oven to 350." Total baking time, one hour precisely. There was another little baking ritual they always performed: about ten minutes before the pasties were to come out of the oven, the ladies made little funnels of brown paper from grocery bags and inserted them into small holes they had left in the top of the crust. Then they poured a spoonful of water into each pasty. Even though the aroma emanating from the finished product was driving the rest of the family into a collective frenzy, the bakers insisted we wait for at least ten minutes after the pasties came out of the oven before the feast could begin.

There was a precise family code of behavior for eating pasties. Utensils were permitted, especially for non-Cornish guests, but the true Cousin Jack or Jennie picked up the pasty and munched slowly down to the end of the treat where, as a culinary coda, the last bit of savory meat juice had collected. No one, not even guests, dared to use condiments on the familial pasties. Even today, close to becoming a septuagenarian, I am revolted when I see diners garnish a pasty with ketchup or, far worse, drown this noble national dish in gravy. Adding other ingredients, carrots, peas or chicken was considered an ethnic sacrilege.

The pasty is a noble and venerable food; as early as 1390, it is mentioned by Jean Frossart and again appears in Shakespeare's *Merry Wives of Windsor* in 1600. The first pasty—called a "hoggan"—was simply a piece of meat, usually pork, wrapped in a lump of dough. The Cornish are accused of putting almost anything into a pie—kidney pies, eel pies, even "star-gazy" pies which consist of small fish (pilchards) which are aligned so that they stare upward at the diner! It is said that the Devil stays away from Cornwall for fear he will be put into a pasty. The pasty was designed as a hearty meal to be carried into the mine to sustain men during the long shifts underground; at dinnertime it was simply heated on a shovel over a candle flame. My Cornish grandfather maintained, with just the hint of a twinkle in his eyes, that the pasties he carried underground were made with barley flour and were so hard they could be dropped down the mine shaft without breaking.

Although I didn't fully understand it at the time, our family ritual of Sunday pasties was one way of connecting us to, and honoring, our heritage. Alas, however, those savory Sunday feasts of authentic Cornish pasties spoiled me forever and only in dire need will I buy one of the ersatz meat pies sold as a genuine ethnic creation.

And so it is I find myself in a bakery, pondering what to do and holding up a line of hungry and impatient autumn tourists, called "leaf-lookers" by the natives. Do I suffer the slings and arrows of disappointment, order a greasy substitute and outrage my tastebuds and my Cornish spirit? Hamlet in a bakery. Impulsively, instead of buying what they promote as a pasty, I grab a bag of saffron buns and flee. I am on a carbohydrate roll anyway—pun intended—and I can munch on a yellow roll as I search out the former Harris family home on Rockland Street.

It's a simple saltbox-style frame building, one of several just like it in a row, constructed long ago by the Calumet and Hecla Company to house their employees. "It cost six dollars a month to rent, dear," my grandmother told me, "and it had five rooms. We heated with coal—the pot-bellied stove was downstairs in the parlor—and we got it from the Company for six dollars a ton. I cooked on a wood-burning range in the kitchen."

Fortunately, my maternal grandparents lived long enough for me to get smart and probe their memories of life in Calumet during the glory years. Loquacious little grandmother did most of the talking as she usually did in any situation, while taciturn grandfather deigned to speak only when he wanted to debate with his wife over some tiny detail. They carried on this form of communication throughout their long married life and, I believe, enjoyed the clashes immensely.

I wanted to learn something about Grandmother Harris' father, my great-grandfather, George Satterly (sometimes spelled Satterley or Satterlee). George was born at the Central mine site in 1866, the third child and first son of Samuel and Eliza Satterly. Like his father, young George went down in the mine to dig copper while still a teenager. Then, when the rich lode of ore played out at Central, he moved to Calumet to work at the even richer copper deposits discovered by the C&H Company.

In Calumet, George Satterly met and married the diminutive Emily Jane Trezona. Emily had come to the Copper Country from Lands End, Cornwall when she was a young girl. Many years later, in the 1940s, when she was an elderly widow, Emily still remembered in vivid detail the stormy passage across the North Atlantic in a sailing schooner. George and Emily had three children: Gertrude, who became my grandmother, another daughter Lucille, and then much later, a son they named George. The boy was adored and indulged by his parents and older sisters. Even a cursory inspection of grave stones in the old Keweenaw cemeteries reveals that children were very vulnerable to disease and infection in those days. Young George had an infected tooth removed and died of blood poisoning in less than four days. When little Georgie died, so did much of the joy in the family.

When my sixteen-year-old grandfather arrived in Calumet after a marathon journey from Cornwall, George Satterly took the young man under his wing. In one of his rare extended narratives, Alfred Harris, my maternal grandfather, spoke about the man who was to become his father-in-law:

> *A lovely man he was. Here I was an overwhelmed lad of sixteen coming to a new job in a new country. But Mr. Satterly (he always referred to his father-in-law as Mr. Satterly) made me feel at home. He even took me into his home to live for a while. That's when your grandmother took a shine to me (Grandmother snorted delicately at this description and let it pass, but I could see her smile).*

> *I worked on his crew, two other lads, both Cornish, Rule and Uren were their names, in Number 5 shaft.*

> *But Mr. Satterly treated me like a son and wanted me to get out of the mine. It was dark, dangerous work, ten hour shifts, six days a week. He didn't have to persuade me much when he found a job for me as a 'grass hand.' That's what they called the men who worked on the surface.*

> *Our job was to cut and get the timbers ready for shoring up the drifts in the mine. The Company used lots of lumber (C.H. used thirty million board feet annually). We had horses for hauling stuff and when the foreman*

reminded me to 'feed the 'orses some hoats and 'ay', it was like being home in St. Austell.

It wasn't all work, you know, Lad. We went to Electric Park (a resort south of town), took buggy rides, had picnics and such. There were at least forty places that sold whiskey and other spirits in town. Sometimes a bunch of us young guys would stand around on a street corner in the evening—what do they call it now? Hanging out? Anyway, this one time we were leaning on the barber pole and it slipped loose and went through the window of Zenith Barber Shop with a hell of a crash!

Did you know we had an earthquake in Calumet one summer? June, no July, I think it was. In 1905.

(Grandmother interrupts, 'July 26, 1906, Al, remember, little Gert, Lon's mother, was just a baby.')

O.K., O.K., Woman. Anyway, after dinner at Mr. Satterly's house ('6:30, Al,' Grandmother adds) there was a big explosion. We thought the bloody powder mill had blown up, or maybe it had been a huge air blast from a hanging wall collapsing in the mine. Those puffs' or 'old rousers' as they called them were really dangerous, they sent a wave of air shooting through the drifts and up the shaft along with lots of dust. They had them all the time at the Quincy; they didn't use much timber over there, just pillars of stone for supporting the ceilings. Anyway, that quake didn't do any damage at the C&H. But the men refused go down the mine shafts for the evening shift.

George Satterly was never quite the same after his little Georgie died. His daughters, young women by then, remembered him taking long solitary walks to deal with his grief. Always a gentle, soft-spoken man, he often withdrew into long periods of silence. Mr. Satterly, as I came to call my great-grandfather after learning more about him, was of medium height and had a slim, wiry build; he had bright blue eyes, a full head of jet black wavy hair and a bushy handlebar moustache.

Underground mining was, and still is, extremely perilous work, and at least one miner was killed in an accident each week on Michigan's copper range. Many more were maimed for life by explosions, falling rock and fires. George Satterly died because a heavy metal pipe fell down a main shaft.

Mr. Satterly and his crew were getting off a man car—a device to transport workers in and out of the mines—at level seven when he heard a distinctive sound: a large metal pipe had broken loose from a cable and was careening down the shaft

Copper miners, late 1800s

Deep in a copper mine

like a missile. Reacting swiftly, Satterly pushed his two young crewmen into the drift. But he was not quick enough to save himself from injury. The heavy pipe cut through his sturdy boot and sliced off his right heel. The wound became infected and my great-grandfather died in agony of tetanus. His death certificate, Number 139, states:

August 27, 1917. George Satterly, miner, died of a mining-related accident.

Mr. Satterly was 51 years, 10 months and 4 days old.

The mining company gave his widow, Emily Jane Satterly, $500 and allowed her to stay in the company-owned house for several weeks. In vivid contrast, Calumet and Hecla paid more than one hundred million dollars in dividends in the period between 1869 and 1915. Most of that fortune went to investors in Boston who celebrated their new wealth by building huge ornate homes and giving lavish endowments to Harvard University. Only a small portion of the money, estimated at 5%, remained in the Keweenaw Peninsula. Some of the *nouveau riche* in Houghton County indulged in displays of conspicuous consumption by erecting mansions in Laurium. The miners, meanwhile, were making $2.50-$3.00 for a ten-hour shift underground in dark, damp and dangerous caverns. I didn't realize how much this glaring disparity between expendable miners and wealthy copper magnates irritated me until my wife and I stayed at the Laurium Manor.

Lynn noticed it first. I was becoming surly and uncommunicative. We had come to Calumet for a Scottish film and feast at the Calumet Theatre hosted by a local club. Instead of driving back home after the event, we elected to stay overnight at the Laurium Manor Mansion Bed and Breakfast. Let me hasten to point out that the present owners have lovingly restored the old mansion and provide an interesting, comfortable and historic place to stay. Just not for me.

Built in 1908 for Thomas Hoatson, Jr., the manor has forty rooms and *13,000* square feet of living space. *13,000 square feet*. The house (palace is a better word) cost $50,000 to build and the new owner spent an additional $35,000 for decorations and furnishings. The music parlor ceiling is inlaid with silver leaf; gilded elephant hide covers the walls in the dining room; velvet curtains frame the windows; a 1,300 square foot ballroom is on the third floor. There are ten bedrooms, two room-sized cedar closets and, I quote from an advertisement, ". . . a grand triple staircase made of hand-carved oak."

The longer we stayed at the manor, the angrier I became. Although the comparison isn't entirely apt, I felt like a descendant of slaves staying at an antebellum mansion in Georgia. I could imagine Tommy rattling around in his trophy home, fondling the elephant hide, admiring the silverleaf, doing an aerobic workout in the ballroom and debating which bedroom to sleep in that night, while my maternal relatives were doing backbreaking work ten hours at a shift in a dark, dank hole, being treated as human machinery and getting paid the munificent sum of 25¢ an hour.

The mine owners knew that labor was cheap and miners were expendable commodities to use up and then discard. A fresh supply of naive and desperate immigrants arrived daily, looking for work. The company officials made it crystal clear: wages and other labor issues were under the exclusive control of Calumet and Hecla. If the workers didn't like it, they could go elsewhere. Looking back, conditions were ripe for the devastating strike of 1913.

A prolonged labor dispute in 1913 was the beginning of the end for the glory days of copper mining on the Keweenaw Peninsula. Encouraged by gains made by unions in the western part of the nation, 13,000 Copper Country miners went out on strike on July 25, 1913. They demanded:

• Better pay. A minimum of at least $3 a day;

• An eight-hour work day;

• Collective bargaining, with the Western Federation of Miners as their bargaining agent;

• Abolition of the one-man drill. To increase worker productivity, Calumet and Hecla officials insisted that the traditional two-man drilling team be abandoned in favor of a new machine that could be operated by one miner. The mine workers countered that the new drill was heavy, difficult to operate and unsafe for one man to work alone.

• Safer working conditions. In 1911, sixty-three men were killed in Keweenaw mining accidents; another 679 workers sustained serious injuries. The union maintained that the companies' obsession with worker efficiency and cost-cutting measures was undermining safety. They pointed out that a man who worked in the mine for one year had a one in two hundred chance of being killed; one of every three experienced an injury. The mining bosses blamed the accidents on careless workers and cited the language barrier involved with so many Finnish, Italian, Slovenian and other non-English-speaking men employed underground.

The Calumet and Hecla Company refused to negotiate with the union and imported laborers to keep the mines going on a token basis. Company officials believed they could wait out the striking miners until economic hardship forced them back into line. The battle lines were drawn. When masses of strikers began assembling at the mines and walking picket lines, violence flared. Since the company managers were intimately involved with all aspects of local government, there was very little delay in firmly recommending to Houghton County Sheriff James Cruse that he petition Michigan governor Woodbridge Ferris to call up the state militia. Cruse was sympathetic to Calumet and Hecla, and ready to do their bidding; soon 2,354 men under the command of Brigadier General Abbey were deployed to patrol the streets and guard the mines. The militia brought with them two batteries of *artillery!* Further inflaming the tense situation, the mining officials also hired private security guards to intimidate the strikers.

The union enlisted well-known advocates of workers' rights, including Mother Jones, John L. Lewis and Clarence Darrow, to speak at rallies and attempt to intervene with the company officials. Calumet and Hecla did not budge. Local merchants, professionals and company sympathizers formed an anti-union Citizens' Alliance and its members wore buttons proclaiming their allegiance. The community was polarized.

The long era of worker exploitation and company paternalism were coming to an end and the company officials were stunned and outraged. After all they had

Superior View Studio, Marquette, MI

Children march during strike

done for the workers—low-cost housing, a library, a bathhouse and more—this strike was the thanks they were getting. The workers countered that Calumet and Hecla paid most of the city taxes and effectively controlled the local government. Whatever C&H wanted, C&H got. The miners were mad as hell and they weren't going to take it anymore.

Similar labor disputes were occurring all over the rapidly industrializing nation. Workers were rising up and demanding a share in the astounding fortunes being made by a few corporate moguls. The garment industry, coal and iron mining, logging—all were going through labor turmoil as the old order was being challenged. It was difficult for the barons to relinquish their rigid control; the managers knew best and would continue to take care of their "children," the workers, as they had always done. Is my characterization a bit overstated? Yes, perhaps. But consider this statement attributed to George F. Baer, chief spokesperson for the mine owners during a Pennsylvania coal strike in 1902:

> "... some people are put on earth to manage, others to serve, and that was the divine order of things. The rights and interests of the laboring man will be protected and cared for, not by labor agitators, but by the Christian men to whom God in his infinite wisdom has given control of the property interests of the country."

As I learned more about the labor dispute on the copper range, I became very curious: what were my relatives, the Satterlys and Harrises, doing during these troubled times? George, Mr. Satterly, did not join the union nor did he stop working in sympathy with the strikers. Cornish folks are very independent by nature and resist joining any cause. Furthermore, as skilled hard rock miners, Cousin Jacks often held the "best" jobs—sinking shafts, extending drifts, chipping ore from the walls. They never picked up the ore or pushed the heavy cars through the drifts to the main shafts. That was the work of the trammers, who usually were Slovenians, Finns and Italians, men who were resentful at what they saw as the favored status of the men from Cornwall.

Grandfather Harris slipped into glacial silence if I brought up the strike. However, I did hear him mutter once that Jim Cruse was fat (the Houghton County sheriff weighed 280 pounds) and incompetent. But my mother and grandmother were more than willing to share their memories of the upheaval in Calumet.

Alfred Harris had no choice of allegiance in the strike: As Undersheriff of Keweenaw County, just north of Calumet, he was allied with the forces for law and order. His job dictated the role he had to play in maintaining peace in the tough little mining locations of Kearsarge, Allouez, Ahmeek. When he was a very elderly man, Grandfather admitted that he was on the wrong side of the labor dispute and that the Company never would have changed its policies without a work stoppage.

Undersheriff Harris' dilemma was compounded by the vacillation of his superior. Grandfather thought that Sheriff John Hepting was temporizing and ineffectual in handling the civil disorder. As an honorary member of the Western Federation of Miners, Hepting's sympathies probably lay with the strikers. As a consequence of the sheriff's ambivalence, Grandfather had to assume more than his share of responsibility in coping with the violence.

The Harris family home became a nightly target of retribution for the arrests Grandfather made. Angry groups of strikers and their families gathered outside the house and shouted insults. Bullets were fired through the windows on several occasions. Mother and her siblings slept on the floor many nights to avoid possible gunfire. Calumet was a powder keg surrounded by a multitude of sparks.

The extreme tension finally exploded into tragedy during the holiday season. On Christmas Eve day, 1913, more than 400 children and 175 adults were attending a party in the Italian Hall on 7th Street in Calumet. The event had been orchestrated by the Women's Auxiliary of the Western Federation of Miners in an attempt to bring a bit of cheer to needy children of the striking miners.

The Italian Hall, *Societa Mutua Beneficenza Italiana*, was located on the upper floor of a brick building; the Vairo Bar and an Atlantic & Pacific Tea Company were located below. The large hall must have been crowded and crackling with excitement. Carols had been sung, recitations made, and now the gifts were going to be distributed. The participants crowded toward the stage at the front of the hall where "Big Annie" Clemenc, a tall, husky Slovenian woman, a firebrand during the picketing, was handing out presents to the children. Just then, someone yelled "Fire!" The excitement about the Christmas gifts segued into panic. The original Italian Hall had burned down on New Years Day, 1908, just five years before. Many of those attending the Christmas Eve party would have remembered it. The guests all tried to flee down the six-foot wide stairwell at the same time. The first few frightened children apparently tripped and fell near the bottom of the twenty-two-step staircase, just before reaching the door. Propelled by the now-contagious panic, scores of others jammed into the clogged stairwell, trampling and crushing those caught beneath the rapidly growing pile of children and adults struggling for their lives. Sixty-two children and eleven adults died of suffocation in the resultant crush. *There had been no fire.*

Who cried fire and triggered the tragedy at the Italian Hall on Christmas Eve? At least one adult attending the party insisted that a man wearing a Citizens' Alliance badge was the culprit but no one was ever indicted by the coroner's jury.

Interior in the Hall as it Appeared the Next Morning

The Italian Hall in Mourning, the Next Day After Disaster

Interior of the Kitchen as it Looked the Next Morning

Bodies of Some of the Victims in One of the Morgues

The Fatal Doorway and Stairs where the People Got Jammed (The Main Entrance Leading to the Hall)

Bodies of Some of the Victims in One of the Morgues

The Town Hall Used as a Temporary Morgue and Where the Inquest Was Held

The Trenches at the Lake View Cemetery where the Victims Were Buried

Some of the Victims in one of the Churches during the Burial Ceremony

"The Italian Hall Disaster in Pictures"

Where 74 People Lost Their Lives in the Christmas Eve Celebration at Calumet, Mich., Dec. 24, 1913, in the Panic of False Cry of "Fire" during Big Strike in Copper Country

The Biggest Catastrophe of its Nature in the History of Michigan

Copyright 1914, A 1 By J. W. Nara Calumet New Studio

Funeral Parade of the Victims Heading to the Cemetery

The Italian Hall tragedy

123

The Funeral Procession, 1913

Residents of the entire copper range were stunned and grief-stricken. An estimated 32,000 people turned out to watch the mournful funeral procession wind its way to the cemetery. My mother, only seven years old at the time, still trembled and wept every time she recalled seeing the grieving miners carry the long line of children's small white coffins through the snowy street. It was a bleak time to be on the Keweenaw Peninsula.

Although the strike ended in April 1914 the community never really recovered from the strife and tragedy. The striking miners lost their struggle. Many residents, including Undersheriff Alfred Harris, moved away from the lingering conflict and deep hatred. The glory years of the Copper Country were over.

On that glum note, I put away the saffron rolls—they had lost their appeal anyway—and drive over to the memorial for the Italian Hall tragedy. The Italian Hall Park was dedicated on November 13, 1989, in memory of the seventy-three children and adults who perished in the disaster on Christmas Eve, 1913. The park features the stone arch that framed the doorway of the Italian Hall and an historic plaque which recounts the incident.

I include now a complete list of the names, ages, sex and national origins of the victims of the tragedy. The list is taken from the 1989 Italian Hall Dedication

Program. Simply citing the number who died there does not do sufficient honor to all the lost human potential. It is important to remember that each of the individuals who perished on that terrible day in 1913 was valued and loved.

List of persons who perished at the Italian Hall on Christmas Eve of 1913

NAME	AGE	RELATIONSHIP	SEX	DESCENT
1. Lempi Ala	12		F	Finnish
2. Herman Alla	60		M	Finnish
3. Sanna J. Aaltonen	39	Mother	F	Finnish
4. Sylvia Aaltonen	3	Daughter	F	Finnish
5. Wilma Altonen	9	Daughter	F	Finnish
6. Will Biri	7		M	Finnish
7. Ivanna Bolf	9		F	Croatian
8. Katarina Bronzo	21		F	Italian
9. Victoria Burcar	9		F	Italian
10. Joseph Butala	7		M	Slovenian
11. Nick Cvetkovick	33		M	Croatian
12. Jenny Giacoletto	9		F	Italian
13. Kararina Gregorich	10		F	Croatian
14. Edwin Heikkinen	7	Brother	M	Finnish
This was his seventh birthday				
15. Eino Felpus O. Heikkinen	10	Brother	M	Finnish
16. Eli Isaac Heikkinen	9	Brother	M	Finnish
17. Ina Isola	33	Mother	F	Finnish
18. Tilma Isola	5	Daughter	F	Finnish
19. Barbara Jesic	25	Mother	F	Croatian
20. Rosie Jesic	5	Daughter	F	Croatian
21. Uno Jokepii	13		M	Finnish
22. Anna E. Kalunki	9	Daughter	F	Finnish
23. Brida Liisa Kalunki	42	Mother	F	Finnish
24. Efia P. Kalunki	8	Daughter	F	Finnish
25. Johan Emil Kiemaki	7		M	Finnish
26. Kararina Klarich	7	Sister	F	Croatian
27. Krishna Klarich	11	Sister	F	Croatian
28. Mary Klarich	9	Sister	F	Croatian
29. Johan Hendrik Koskela	10		M	Finnish

NAME	AGE	RELATIONSHIP	SEX	DESCENT
30. Anna Kotajarvi	4	Daughter	F	Finnish
31. Anna Kotajarvi	39	Mother	F	Finnish
32. Mary Krainatz	11		F	Croatian
33. Hilja K. Lanto	5	Daughter	F	Finnish
34. Maria G. Lanto	40	Mother	F	Finnish
35. Sulo Rubet Lauri	8		M	Finnish
36. Mary Lesar	13	Sister	F	Slovenian
37. Rafael Lesar	2	Brother	M	Slovenian
38. Arthur Lindstrom	12		M	Swedish
39. Lydia Johanna Luoma	10		F	Finnish
40. Alfred J. W. Lustic	7		M	Finnish
41. Elina Manley	26	Mother	F	Finnish
42. Wesley Manley	4	Son	M	Finnish
43. Ella E. Mantanen	8	Sister	F	Finnish
44. Mathias E. Mantanen	10	Brother	F	Finnish
45. Yrja H. Mantanen	13	Brother	M	Finnish
46. Agnes Mihelchich	7	Cousin	F	Croatian
47. Elizabeth Milelchich	9	Cousin	F	Croatian
48. Paul Milelchich	5	Cousin	M	Croatian
49. Walter Murto	9		M	Finnish
50. Edward Emil Myllykangas	7	Brother	M	Finnish
51. Johan W. Myllykangas	10	Brother	M	Finnish
52. Abram Niemela	24	Husband	M	Finnish
53. Maria Elizabeth Niemela	22	Wife	F	Finnish
54. Annie Papesh	6	Sister	F	Finnish
55. Mary Papesh	14	Sister	F	Slovenian
56. Kate Petteri	66		F	Finnish
57. Saida M. Raja	10		F	Finnish
58. Terresa Renaldi	12		F	Italian
59. Elma W. Ristel	6		F	Finnish
60. Emilia Rydilahti	16	Sister	F	Finnish
61. Heli Rydilahti	13	Sister	F	Finnish
62. John Saari	5		M	Finnish
63. Elida Saatio	1		F	Finnish
64. Mary Smuk	5		F	Slovenian
65. Antonia Staudohar	7		F	Croatian/ Slovenian
66. Elisina J. Taipalus	6	Sister	F	Finnish

NAME	AGE	RELATIONSHIP	SEX	DESCENT
67. Sandra M. Taipalus	4	Sister	F	Finnish
68. Edward Richard Takola	9		M	Finnish
69. Lydia E. Talpaka	10		F	Finnish
70. Kaisa G. Tulppo	45	Mother	F	Finnish
71. Mamie L. Tulppo	10	Daughter	F	Finnish
72. Hilja Wualukka	8		F	Finnish
73. Johan Peter Westola	48		M	Finnish

It is early afternoon and my spirits revive a bit in the autumn sun. Still, I cannot bring myself to leave Calumet with the ghostly images lingering in my thoughts. There is time, I can *take* the time—after all this is my journey—to meet the elderly gentleman I had been encouraged to visit while in town.

"John will charm and amaze you," Dean Premo predicted. It's time to be amazed and charmed, I think, as I head for Caledonia Street.

It has been said so often that it has become a cliche: "Everybody has a story." Sure, sure. But then you meet a modest man living in a modest home on a modest street in a small town in northern Michigan and you are totally overwhelmed by the tale he shares.

John Perona is eighty-two years old, bald and hobbled a bit by arthritis. When I shake hands with him, I notice that his palm is wet. He smiles. "I was cleaning house when you arrived," he explains. Despite my prior phone call and a follow-up letter, John still is not sure why I want to meet with him. When I mention music, Dean Premo and *White Water* Family Band, John relaxes a bit. But he still wonders.

"I'm just a simple man with an eighth-grade education. I've been a laborer all my life. Why would people be interested in me?"

When I mumble something about my journey to Central and talking with people along the way, John moves closer. Very close.

"I'm hard of hearing," he says and smiles again. Not only does John Persona have a wonderful smile, he is a very good listener. Perhaps his hearing loss requires that he pay close attention, but I would wager he has always been interested in and attentive to what others have to say.

Born to immigrant Italian parents, John grew up on a farm near Calumet. An observant child, he became interested in the natural world, particularly the moths and butterflies which fluttered about the farm fields while he hoed the corn or did other chores. One Christmas, an older sister gave him a book on identifying butterflies and started his lifelong obsession with insects.

John Perona, a man of moths and music

Calumet Theatre

The Italian Arch

"Would you like to see my collection?" John asks shyly. Indeed I would. Leading me into his cluttered living room John points to five large cabinets.

"I made those for my insect display," he said, opening one cabinet and pulling out a tray, "And all these trays, too." I notice a strong odor of mothballs. John explains that in order to protect his mounted specimens from being ravished by live insects, it is necessary to use lots of moth crystals.

The insect collection is astounding! John shows me tray after tray of butterflies and moths under glass, all neatly displayed and labeled. I marvel at the lovely green luna and the dark brown-and-white cecropia, species I had learned about and collected in my high school years. Midway through inspection of various types of beetles, I have to leave abruptly to get some fresh air. The mothballs are overwhelming my respiratory system. John is concerned and follows me out on his porch where I am coughing and wheezing.

"I don't notice the smell anymore," John says, "Maybe the mothballs are the reason why I'm so well-preserved."

As he removes the last tray from the last cabinet, I ask, "How many specimens do you have, John?"

"More than six thousand," he says modestly.

Six thousand insects! A world-class collection, worthy of a major university and all accomplished by one person as an avocation.

"Some colleges in Michigan are interested in my collection," John tells me in his quiet, almost diffident manner. I bet they are!

Noticing a music stand in the corner of the parlor, I inquire if John plays an instrument.

"I play the bones," he says, picking up a box and showing me two pieces of ebony. "But these are really wood." Then he begins to click the dark sticks and John Perona is transformed right before my eyes. Starting slowly with a percussive clack, he increases the speed into a marvelous rhythm. As he plays, the years fall away. His face loses twenty, thirty, forty and more years of wear and wrinkles and his torso and legs move youthfully to the beat. John looks and moves like the young man he had been. I don't want to interrupt the illusion and motion for him to continue. In a final flourish, he clicks out the old cadence, "Shave and a haircut, two bits."

Then John picks up two large metal spoons. He had flattened the bowl of one to enhance the sound when they are clicked together. And what divine sounds he makes! As the tintinnabulation continues on and on, I think of Edgar Allen Poe's poem about bells.

"I also play the concertina," John says. It is very difficult for me to break the spell but it is time for me to leave. I am going back to Central and I had best get on with my journey. John seems reluctant to see me go and suggests, "I could go with you, be your guide. I've been all over this country collecting my insects." It is tempting. But this trip to Central is a very personal pilgrimage and I must visit my Cornish ancestors alone. Promising that I will return, I say goodbye to the remarkable John Perona. Everybody *does* have a story.

NINE

The sun is slanting toward the southwest and I am only eighteen miles from Central. This is one of my favorite portions of the journey. I drive through several small villages, all former mine locations. There is not a lot to see, really—a rusting shaft house there, piles of dark waste rock everywhere, and rows of identical company houses. But I always sense the energy and spirit of the men and women who lived and worked here during the golden years of the Copper Country.

The names of the villages intrigue me:

Kearsarge, named for the good ship, U.S.S. *Kearsarge*. I salute the stone replica docked in the center of town.

Copper City. In an open election the local residents selected Copper City over Ulseth, Finneganville or Agassiz. A good choice.

Allouez is named for the Jesuit priest, Father Claude Jean Allouez, thought to be the first white man to see the rich copper deposits on the Keweenaw Peninsula.

Ahmeek. My favorite. Named for the large rodent which was the impetus for opening the north country to exploration and altered many native cultures forever. The land around this community was wet and boggy, so the residents got together and probably said, "What the heck, let's call this benighted town Ahmeek, an Indian word (*Ahmuk*) for beaver." See what I mean about the spirit of these pioneers? Once a thriving community with a theatre, two schools, a bakery and regular trolley service, Ahmeek is now a sleepy hamlet. A black and white dog is lying out in the middle of one of the main streets when I go through!

Mohawk was named by one Ernest Koch, a lumberman, who found deposits of copper during his rambles in the woods. The name derives from a Native American word for "bear." Here's a bit of trivia: In 1910, a local cricket team won the Copper Country pennant. Let's hear it for the Mohawk Ursines!

North of Mohawk, the last settlement of any size, U.S. Highway 41 winds through dense forests of maple, aspen and conifer. This route is very old. Prehistoric indigenous peoples carried copper, laboriously dug from open pits, along an ancient path here; they traded the metal to other natives in Ohio, Illinois, Indiana and places even further south. Then, in the seventeenth and eighteenth centuries, French explorers, missionaries and fur traders passed this way. Close behind, starting in the mid-1800s, hundreds of copper miners used the route in search of the red metal. The federal government constructed a military road on this pathway, all the way from an army outpost, Fort Wilkins, at Copper Harbor to Fort Howard, near the present-day city of Green Bay, Wisconsin. Eventually, loggers moved in to harvest the vast timber resources of pine and hardwood. With much of the dense forest cut off and the terrain opened, a few hardy settlers tried to farm and coax a living from the flinty land.

Today, this historic pathway is traversed mainly by summer tourists on their way to Eagle River, Eagle Harbor, Brockway Mountain Drive and—the end of the road—Copper Harbor. And by a few wanderers like me, to paraphrase Kent Nerburn, seeking to connect the undeniable tension between the forgotten past and a familiar present.

There are distinctive and very delightful wooden place signs in Keweenaw County, and I notice one now announcing the site of an old Catholic cemetery for the former town of Clifton. According to local lore, the first really large copper lode was discovered here when John Hayes, a Pittsburgh pharmacist, slid down a cliff and barked his derriere on a piece of projecting copper. When shafts were sunk deep into the greenstone, massive deposits of amygdaloid copper were found within the lava flows; in this formation, the metal was found in cohesive masses, some as small as raisins, others in great chunks weighing tons.

The experienced miners, recent immigrants from Cornwall, were astounded by the giant boulders of pure copper.* They soon found out that it was difficult and time-consuming to break these massive chunks into pieces small enough to get up the mine shaft. The Cliff Mine produced more than forty million pounds of copper and delivered two and one-half million dollars before the rich vein ran out.

While the ore lasted, Clifton was a very active village. In 1866, a thousand people lived here; there were three churches, a school and several fraternal organizations. Father Baraga preached here, as did the Methodist Reverend John Pitezel of L'Anse. The school master, Vermonter Henry Hobart, came to the village in 1865. He was responsible for 150 children, then called "scholars," and clearly was disgruntled to find himself in a rude frontier village. In his diary he complained that Cliff was the "most Godforsaken place in the country" with hordes of mosquitoes, blackflies and other biting insects. Hobart disliked the Cornish people too, considering them coarse, dirty, rough and intemperate in the use of liquor. He wrote

---

*In the summer of 2000, a seventeen-ton copper boulder was found in Lake Superior near Eagle River and is now on display at the Quincy Mine location.

that "the head of most any child was infested with enough lice to make a Cornish pasty." * At least old Hank had a sense of humor even if he was a bit stiff-necked.

Just down the road from the Cliff Cemetery, I pass by Phoenix, another boom-and-bust mining location. First operated by the Lake Superior Copper Company in 1845, the town reached its nadir with about a thousand residents in 1880. In addition to mass copper deposits, the miners found silver at this site; a silver nugget weighing eight-and-three-quarter pounds was unearthed.

I can tell I am dawdling along these last few miles, postponing and savoring the anticipation of reaching Central. Instead of a silver nugget, I locate gold—an extensive patch of my favorite flower, goldenrod—growing by the roadside near Central Creek. In late summer, I look forward to the waves of bright yellow decorating all the highways and abandoned fields. Many years ago, enamored of the simple beauty of the goldenrod plant, I looked up the flower in various botanical references. After I discovered that there are some sixty-nine varieties, and that it is often difficult to tell one from the other, I decided I would rather spend my time admiring its beauty than keying down which variety I happened to be adoring at the moment.

And now the moment I have been looking forward to all day—I am back to Central. As I pause at the entrance road to the old town, I can almost hear my grandfather say, "This is the one we've been looking for, Lad."

Central. Section 23, Township 58N, Range 31W. No one knows why the mining community was called Central, although it may have been because it was located between two older mines, the Winthrop and the North Western. Also called Central Mine, the town had a relatively short existence; it was born in 1854, died in 1898. But it was a lively place, as a historical marker at the entrance to the former town attests:

> In 1854 heavy masses of native copper were discovered at the bottom of an ancient pit dug by prehistoric miners. In November of that year the Central Mining Company was organized. A rich ore body was soon opened which had produced a total of $9,770,628 by July 1898 when the property was finally abandoned. Until the Kearsarge Lode was discovered in the 1890s, the Central Mine was the biggest and most profitable producer in the Keweenaw District. At one time the population reached a total of approximately 1,250 people, and reunions of former residents are held here annually.

---

*Philip Mason, ed. *Copper Country Journal: The Diary of Schoolmaster Henry Hobart, 1863-1864.*

Central is located in Keweenaw County, the northernmost tip of the copper-laden peninsula. The county lies closer to the North Pole than does Quebec, Canada, and has an average annual snowfall of 265 inches. Although it is the least populous county in the State of Michigan and has the smallest county seat, Eagle River, it has the longest, most beautiful shoreline—eighty-four miles of high cliffs, pebbled beaches and tall sand dunes. The ghost town of Central drowses on the southeastern slope of the greenstone ridge that extends the full length of the Keweenaw Peninsula; the site commands a magnificent view of Mt. Bohemia and Mt. Houghton almost twelve miles away near the shore of Lake Superior. Almost directly south of Central an Air Force radar base used to crouch ominously atop Mt. Horace Greeley. The former base site is now occupied by a youth training facility.

Parking the Silver Shrike under a brilliant red maple tree, I saunter slowly down the street to inspect the old houses still standing. Although a few residents live here throughout the year, most of the houses are owned now by people who use them for summer homes. I pause to rest and reflect on the front steps of one abandoned home. Whose house this is, I cannot tell, but he will not mind that an old Cousin Jack has come back to Central to visit his ancestors.

Is that just the murmur of the breeze in the trees or did I hear the Cornish word, *Dynnargh*, meaning "welcome?" Leaning back against a post, I summon up the ghosts of Central: the rasping oaths uttered by weary miners as they climb the endless ladders from the depths of the mine; the heavy sighs of dispirited women as they stare from frost-rimmed windows on a frigid January morning; the peal of the school bell summoning the reluctant scholars back to class after lunch on a balmy spring afternoon; the faint echo of the Silver Coronet Band practicing on the village green; Cornish voices raised in glorious harmony at the Methodist Episcopal church. When I close my eyes and concentrate, I can even smell pasties baking and tea being brewed for the evening meal.

This was Cornish Country. In fact, Central was sometimes called "Little Cornwall" since so many residents hailed from that small county in the far west of England. But no one dared call a Cousin Jack or Cousin Jennie *English*. At least not to their faces. They were Cornish and very proud of their Celtic heritage. The rocky peninsula of Cornwall juts out into the Atlantic Ocean like a lobster claw and its stony ramparts may account for its name. The prefix *Corn* refers to a geographic feature, the rocky coastal promontories in Cornwall. The *wall* part of the name probably refers to an Anglo-Saxon word for the original, indigenous British natives; the word *walas* or *wealas*, for example, is the forerunner of Wales. Thus, we have Cornwall, the land of the *Britons of Corn*. In the veins of the Cornish courses the blood of King Arthur, ancient lord of Tintagel, now a ruined castle near the Camelford River on the northern coast of Cornwall. Camelford, could it be

Camelot? The proud people of this land beside the sea think so.

When the Romans invaded the British Isles, the Celtic tribes retreated to rocky redoubts in Wales, Scotland and Cornwall and refused to adopt the culture of the conquerors. I understood this fiery independence better when I traveled in Britain. As the train crossed over the Tamar River from Devon to Cornwall, a large billboard near the tracks proclaimed, "You are now leaving England and entering Cornwall."

The Cornish are the greatest miners in the world. It was commonly observed that wherever there is a hole in the earth, you will find a Cornishman at the bottom of it. So it was inevitable that hundreds of Cornishmen were recruited to work the new copper mines in the Keweenaw Peninsula. For centuries the sturdy residents of Cornwall had worked deep underground in search of tin and copper in their native country. The men from Cornwall knew the dangers and drudgery of mining and accepted each new challenge with typical Celtic enthusiasm.

Even so, Central must have been an awesome challenge to the early miners and their families. Consider the conditions that confronted them: the isolation of being many miles by stage coach from a town of any size; sickness, particularly childhood diseases such as diphtheria, which swept through communities claiming the lives of scores of children; accidents in the mine which maimed and killed many; crowded living conditions in the boarding houses where beds were used around the clock by miners working on different shifts; and the long, cold winters. Scratched on a windowpane in the home of the mining clerk, now tastefully and authentically restored, is the terse inscription: Feb. 8, '88, 54 below. It was to this remote mining village that my great-great-grandfather came in 1860.

Samuel Satterly was born on May 3rd in the year 1836. Although he had a Devonshire surname, his mother Ann Medland was partly Cornish and the family lived in Cornwall where Samuel's father William was a miner. Most Cornish last names begin with a limited number of prefixes, to wit this common expression:

By Tre-, Ros-, Pol-, Lan-, Car-, and Pen-
You may know most Cornishmen

In order, these prefixes translate: a *town*, a *hearth*, a *pool*, a *church*, a *castle* or *city* and a *promontory* or *headland*.

I don't know anything about Samuel's childhood, but as a teenager he worked on a farm in Devon. He appears on the 1860 census as a young man working in the Minesota Mine (The clerk who registered the claim couldn't spell worth a darn) in Rockland, a small town at the extreme south end of the Keweenaw copper deposits. Samuel and his teenage cousin, John, had sailed by clipper ship from the Old Country to seek their fortunes in the wilds of the Upper Peninsula.

Both young Satterlys left the Rockland area abruptly in late 1860, either because of violence between the Cornish and Irish or because they were lured by better opportunities in the north. The Irish and Cornish were noted for their bloody battles. Liquor no doubt was involved, as well as the volatile Celtic propensities of both ethnic groups, but most of the animosity stemmed from the fact that the lads from Cornwall were expert miners. While the Cousin Jacks were performing tasks that called for hard rock mining skills, the Irish were relegated to menial labor. Tempers flared into homicide on April 24, 1859, when Dan Ryan killed John Terrill with an axe blow to the head. A large group of angry Cornish miners rampaged through Rockland seeking revenge on any Irishman they encountered.

I expect, though, that Samuel was lured north by his uncle, George Satterly, who had been hired on as clerk at Central Mine, a prestigious position in the mining operation. The rich new mine had turned a neat profit in its very first year. Samuel and John, who would later end up at the Quincy Mine, boarded a coastal packet boat and sailed to Eagle Harbor. Landing in the beautiful natural harbor on Lake Superior, the young Cornishmen then hiked the six miles to Central on a rudimentary tote road carved through the dense forest. What did they think as they trudged through the deep, dark woods? Would they have agreed with Schoolcraft when he commented about the tip of the Keweenaw Peninsula, "One cannot help fancying that he has gone to the ends of the earth and beyond the boundaries appointed by the residence of man." *

The two young Satterly men arrived at the James Rowe boarding house just in time for afternoon tea and heavy cake. Almost immediately they felt at home in a residence where everyone spoke with a Cornish brogue and had familiar Cornish names: Rule, Curnow, Trewhella, Trudgeon, Chenoweth, Pendray, Polglaze and Uren. Samuel and John learned that they would have to share a bed with a miner working a different shift; although thirty-six miners lived at the boarding house, there were only eighteen beds. While one miner worked a ten-hour day shift, another worker assigned to the night shift would sleep. Then, when the day shift miner got back to the house, the same bed was his for the night. The sheets never got cold. Neither did the bedbugs.

Life in the boarding house was spartan. With no central heat, just a stove in the parlor and a wood-burning range in the kitchen, the bedrooms were frigid in the winter. The mattresses were lumpy pads of straw, barley straw being a favorite. Each bedroom had a chamber set: small wash stand, basin, a pitcher of water, one stringy towel and a chamber pot for bathroom needs.

---

*Henry Rowe Schoolcraft, *Narrative journal...*, Michigan State College Press, 1953.

Houghton County Historical Society, Lake Linden, Mi

Early days at Central

Food, while usually abundant, was definitely lacking in variety. But the men were so famished after their shift in the mine, all they cared about was filling their stomachs as swiftly as possible. The cook did not have to fuss with how the meal was presented; she just put the platters on the table and got out of the way. After dinner the men gathered in the parlor, smoked their pipes, chatted a bit and headed to bed to restore themselves for the next day's work.

Let's follow young Samuel Satterly as he goes about his work underground. The year is 1867. The State of Nebraska is admitted to the Union. The U.S. Senate agrees to buy Alaska. Horatio Alger publishes his novel, *Ragged Dick*, a portrayal of the American Dream.

Promptly at six a.m., Sam enters the dry house to get ready for his ten-hour shift in the mine. The dry house, commonly called the "dry," was where the miners could clean up after a work day and store their grimy clothes. Changing into rough pants, coat and boots, Sam places a fresh bit of clay on his hat and sticks a large candle into the gooey blob. Clutching his round metal lunch pail, he descends a series of ladders into Number 2 shaft; his three team members climb down close behind him. Samuel's team has contracted with the mining captain, James Dunstan, to produce so many pounds of ore in a specified period of time.

Other men descending into the black depths begin to sing and soon the wonderful harmony of Cornish voices echoes and re-echoes in the shaft. This habit of

Cornish miners to sing as they went about their work probably spawned the legend of Dick Buller. Dick Buller's powerful bass voice, the story goes, could penetrate ten levels in the mine. On the surface, it was said that his singing was so loud it could be heard miles away. One Sunday morning, just as the congregation was emerging from church service in Mandan, ten miles north of Central, Dick Buller's melodious bellow soared through the forest, enveloping the worshipers. The preacher fell to his knees and shouted, "Praise the Lord! Gabriel has come!"

Arriving at their assigned place in the drift at the 4th level, 240 feet below the surface, Sam and his team members stick their candles in a convenient crevice in the rocky wall. With only the feeble light of four candles, the young men will spend their day working in pairs, hammering, chiseling and shoveling the heavy ore. The men will mine using the "retreat system." In this method, drifts are extended off the main shaft a certain distance, and the workers dig for ore back toward the shaft, instead of mining while advancing away from the shaft. The miners preferred the retreat system, believing it was safer.

The air is stale and filled with fine metallic dust. With each breath, the men inhale the particles deep into their lungs. Samuel's team did not bring a caged bird with them this day, but many miners did carry a canary down into the mine. Birds are very susceptible to a deficit of oxygen or to toxic air; when the canary began to flutter in its cage, the miners knew that it was time to flee.

At midmorning, Sam notices a flickering light approaching in the drift. As the human figure gets closer, the men can see that he is clad in white and makes a stark contrast against the dark walls. That would be the mining captain coming to check on how the men are faring at their work.

"'ere comes Cap'n Jim, Lads," Sam announces. Almost in unison the four miners stop working; this was common practice among Cornish miners. If they had been taking a break from their heavy labors, they would have remained seated. Somehow, perhaps by example or precept, I must have absorbed the Cornish workman's code from my grandfather; while employed at various summer jobs during my college years, I always stopped working when the supervisor approached.

When it is about noon, the young miners stack the tools and retrieve their lunch pails. Two of the men have pasties, and they heat the meal-in-a-crust on a shovel over a candle. As they reach in their pockets for a small tobacco pouch, smiles punctuate their grimy faces: they found some silver intermingled with the free copper this morning. Carefully, they chip out the small nuggets of silver in the "half-breeds," as they call the clumps of mixed copper and silver, and put them in the pouches they always carry for this purpose. While the owners and stockholders would sternly disapprove of the men purloining silver in *their* mines, the mining captains look the other way. After all, the men were hired to mine *copper*, and if they happened upon other metal during their work, well, finder's keepers.

One of the young miners begins to hum a familiar tune and soon all four workers are belting out a lusty rendition of "Trelawny," the national anthem of Cornwall. In 1698, Sir Jonathon Trelawny protested a royal edict and was imprisoned in the Tower of London. Thousands of irate Cornishmen rallied to his cause and marched on London demanding Trelawny's release. Eventually he was acquitted and released. Reverend Robert Hawker wrote this stirring call to arms:

Trelawny

A good sword and a trusty hand,
A merry heart and true
King James' men shall understand
What Cornish lads can do
And have they fixed the where and when
And shall Trelawny die?
Here's twenty thousand Cornish men
Will know the reason why.
(Chorus)
And shall Trelawny live?
Or shall Trelawny die?
Here's twenty thousand Cornish men
Will know the reason why!
Out spake their captain brave and bold
A merry wight was he,
If London's Tower were Michael's Hold
We'd set Trelawny free.
We'll cross the Tamar land to land,
The Severn is no stay,
With "One and All" and hand in hand,
And who will bid us nay?
(Chorus)
And when we come to London Wall
A pleasant sight to view,
Come forth! Come forth, ye cowards all!
Here's men as good as you.
Trelawny he's in keep and hold,
Trelawny he may die,
Here's twenty thousand Cornish bold
Will know the reason why!

Near the end of their shift, Samuel Satterly and his three co-workers carry out one last task: they drill holes in the rock to prepare for blasting. Carefully, black powder is tamped into the holes and fuses are set. Close to the 4 p.m. quitting time, controlled explosions loosen tons of rock in the drifts. Two hours later, when the evening shift reports for work, the main shaft and all the drifts will be relatively clear of dust.

Finally, the men make the onerous climb up the series of ladders to the surface. There is no singing now. Weary and breathless, the miners inch upward, ladder-rung after ladder-rung, toward the light. The young men recover a bit, then wash off the grime and change clothes in the dry. There is time for some joking and teasing.

"Well, the 'knackers' didn't get us today, Lads," one older miner observes. Miners, particularly Cornish miners, tended to be superstitious and, when things went wrong underground, they often blamed the little spirits (sometimes called "piskeys" or, in Cornish, *Pobel Vyghan*) which haunt the depths.

"Not today, aye, my friend," says another mature miner. "I've got ashes from the fire last night in me pocket to keep the wee folk away."

Sam and his workmates trudge toward the boarding house. They did not want to be late for supper. The men needed to rest and restore for the next day's labor. And the next.

Every day was a work day except Sunday, when the entire village of Central observed the Sabbath. One building stands out among all the somber weathered houses at Central: the old Methodist Episcopal Church. The Cornish were serious about their religion—John Wesley saw to that during his many crusades in Cornwall—and the miners, with the financial help of the mining company, built a very sturdy church in 1868. The well-kept frame building sits on a stone foundation which extends out from a sloping hillside; its simple square steeple is shaped like the crown of Henry VIII. Since 1907, the church has served as the site of an annual reunion for the descendants of the original residents of Central. When I attended one of the reunions a few years ago as a fifth-generation descendant of a Cornish copper miner, I liked to believe that I sat in the very same narrow wooden pew where Samuel Satterly worshiped so long ago.

The Central Mining Company recognized that they needed a stable, reliable workforce and that single men living in spartan boarding houses would not provide it. Consequently, they started building houses to rent to married miners. Tiring of life in a crowded boarding house and lonely for his sweetheart in the Old Country, Samuel sent for his very own Cousin Jennie.

A typical company home in Central

Eliza Chewidden (means "white or light-colored house"). Isn't that a delightful name for a great-great grandmother? Can't you just see her arriving in remote Central, all colorful and frilly in a pink bonnet and a long gingham dress? Did she have a sense of humor and anticipate a line from another Eliza, the flower girl urchin in *My Fair Lady* and say to Sam when they met, "I washed my face and 'ands, I did"?

What did the simple folks do in Central to escape the numbing dailiness of work and survival in the wilderness? They took buggy rides to Eagle River and Eagle Harbor, attended performances of the local band, went on picnics, attended church socials and gathered in each other's homes for food, music and camaraderie. The men enjoyed membership in fraternal organizations; Samuel belonged to the Sons of St. George, as did many Cornishmen. The ladies got together for quilting and sewing parties.

There was a large, well-stocked company store and several small shops—shoe repair, butcher shop and candy store. There were no saloons—no saloons!—at Central, but I have it on the best authority that some Cornishmen brought recipes for their favorite libations from the Old Country. Here is one for mead (*metheglin* in Cornish), a traditional wine made from honey. Newlyweds were given a jug of mead for the first month of their marriage, hence the expression, "honeymoon."

The ingredients:
- *four pounds honey*
- *one gallon water*

Boil the mixture of honey and water for one hour, then skim

- *add one ounce of hops*

Boil for 50 minutes; let the mixture sit for a day, then bottle

I don't know if Samuel Satterly hunted or fished but game was plentiful around the village. As an inveterate birder, I envy the fact that he probably saw vast flocks of passenger pigeons, a bird which became extinct in 1914. It seems, though, that Sam and Eliza must have spent considerable time making and raising children.

Large families were the norm in those early days, and the young Satterly couple did their duty to uphold the numbers. They had fourteen children: Eveline, George (my great-grandfather), Mary Etta, Thomas, Maud, Clara, Charley, Will and Samuel; five children died in childbirth or as infants. Many youngsters died of croup, diphtheria, scarlet fever, influenza and other illnesses that now are almost eliminated.

Life in a frontier town must have been very challenging for women. Simply doing laundry must have been backbreaking work, particularly in winter. Preserving food, cooking and sewing for a large family was almost a full-time job. The harsh climate, lack of hygiene and inadequate medical attention all took their toll. When Lynn and I visited an overgrown cemetery near the old Cliff Mine, we happened upon one particular gravestone which revealed a poignant picture of life in the nineteenth century. The stone, shaped into an obelisk, memorialized a family. On each of three stone sides was etched the name and dates of a child lost to the family in infancy: Ella, five months old, died September 16, 1865; William, ten months old, died April 29, 1867; Catherine, five months old, died July 5, 1974. On the fourth side was the name of the young mother, Jane Peters, who died at age thirty-one on June 28, 1874, seven days before baby Catherine.

The women who survived had to be tough and enduring; they had to get up very early each day, stoke the fire, sweep the floor and scrape together a meal for their families. The women who persevered had steel in their spines and, quite often, a direct and earthy approach to life. My little grandmother Harris was the essence of feisty and earthy; even after I was married and had children of my own, she pointedly asked if my bowels were regular. When I mentioned this earthiness attribute to Dean Premo, he laughed and told me this tale about his own Cornish grandmother:

After much delay, Mrs. Premo had to go to the dentist to see about an aching tooth. Reluctantly she entered the treatment room and sat down in the leather reclining chair. A dental assistant put a paper bib in place and then Dr. Wilkins appeared. After some perfunctory conversation, the dentist readied a drill. Mrs. Premo reached back and grasped the dentist's testicles in her strong right hand. Dr. Wilkins almost shrieked, "Mrs. Premo! You have a hold of my testicles and if you were to squeeze, it would really hurt!" After a brief pause for dramatic effect, Mrs. Premo responded, "Yes, doctor, and let's make sure that neither one of us gets hurt today."

While none of my maternal relatives characterized Samuel Satterly as earthy, my grandmother Harris, my mother and aunts all said that he was a bit of a comedian. He liked to make people laugh, a trait I share. As in my own case, some of Sam's co-workers thought he was pretty silly. Alex Haley, the author of *Roots*, wrote that when we look back at our forebears, we often find someone who is a lot like us. Apparently, Grandfather Sam and I share a number of traits.

Samuel was described as very intuitive, almost impulsive in temperament. He made up his mind quickly. His granddaughters reported that he seemed to relish getting himself almost, but not quite, into trouble by things he said or did. That troublemaker trait in myself has bemused and amused me for more than half-a-century.

So does the Satterly tendency to laugh when untoward events occur. In response to many situations, we always seem to find something funny, some silly incongruity to lighten the seriousness. This familial trait, the ability to put people at ease with humor, I consider an asset. It can also be a great liability when employed with the wrong person or in an inappropriate situation.

Interestingly, Grandfather Satterly and I also share a counterpoint to humor: the tendency to nostalgia and melancholy. This provocative blending of mirth and melancholy is common to persons of Celtic heritage, such as the Welsh, Irish and Cornish. If we were not joking and laughing, we might be weeping.

Celts are also tuned into the natural world, almost mystically so. In fact, a cornerstone of Celtic spirituality is an ardent relationship with the geography where they live; each rock, hill and stream take on a special significance in daily life. Grandfather Satterly loved the land of his birth and transferred that affection to the Upper Peninsula. If you have been paying attention, you are already well aware that the author shares this passion for place.

When I was coming of age in the late 1940s, and showing a strong interest in young females, my mother told me one day that I was just like Grandfather Sam.

When I asked what she meant, she replied cryptically, "Your great-great grandfather was a 'ladies' man,'" and would not elaborate. No one ever accused Samuel of infidelity—no rogue he; they just acknowledged that he liked the company of women, that he had a knack for making ladies feel they were interesting and valued. Thanks a lot for that genetic endowment, Grandfather Sam. Mentoring young women and enjoying the friendship of scores of others has made all the difference in my life.

I too enjoy—in fact prefer—the company of women. I like the way they think, the way they talk, and the fact that women can express feelings without the loss of esteem I often find among my male friends. It is also comforting to be in the presence of the gender that does not have the need to "rooster," to be stronger, faster, smarter, and to put down their peers with zingers. Thanks again, Sam.

Great-great grandfather Satterly was devoted to sweets, especially baked goods, as am I. We also share an addiction to licorice. I was in late middle-age when I discovered this similarity in food preferences by scanning Sam's purchases in the old record book of the Central Company Store. Eureka! Now I finally learned the origin of the nickname—"Sugary Sam"—given to me by my mother and grandmother.

All my maternal relatives agreed that Samuel Satterly was deeply ashamed that he could not read or write. Never was he more embarrassed than when he declared his intent to become a citizen of the United States. On August 19, 1869, Samuel swore to "renounce forever all allegiance and fidelity to each and every Foreign Prince, Potentate, State or Sovereignty whosoever, particularly the Queen of England of whom I have been a subject." The clerk signed Sam's name and between the Samuel and Satterly, great-great-grandfather placed his mark, an **X**. Many of the men and women at Central were not literate, and they vowed that their children would not be limited in the ways they themselves had been. Their children would do better and, in order to do that, they needed to build a school.

Although formal schooling for the children started not long after the mining operation began, in 1878 the community erected a fine new school building; it was an impressive monument to the residents' faith in education and the future of their children. The school was designed with three stories and its $7,500 cost was a considerable sum for those times. The building had a mansard roof, large windows and an entrance with an attractive portico. The top floor was used as a hall for town meetings, social events and the arts, while the lower two floors were divided into four rooms for the grade school. During the height of the mining operation, more than two hundred children attended classes in the new school. Although nothing remains of the large structure, I like to think that the mental ripples created by teachers and pupils there years ago still echo outward in the lives of their descendants and that perhaps my own modest literary achievements had their origin in a kerosene-lit school in Central.

Declaration of Intention.

COPY.

STATE OF MICHIGAN, ss.

County of Keweenaw,

The District Court for said County, to wit:

I, *Samuel Satterly*

do solemnly swear that it is bona fide my intention to become a **CITIZEN OF THE UNITED STATES,** *and to* **RENOUNCE FOREVER** *all allegiance and fidelity to each and every Foreign Prince, Potentate, State or Sovereignty whatsoever, and particularly the Queen of England of whom I have been a subject.*

Sworn to and Subscribed before me, at

_____ *this* _____ *day of* _____

A. D. 186__ _____ Clerk.

(Signed,) *Samuel X Satterly*

Mark

Samuel Satterly's American citizenship paper

By the mid-1880s, the rich copper lode was running out and the production at the Central Mining Company was dwindling. Many miners left to seek work at the booming Calumet and Hecla operation. Samuel and Eliza took their children and followed their fellow workers to the bustling town of Calumet.

Starting over in a new town with a much larger and ethnically diverse population, a lively business district which included several saloons and a burgeoning new mining company was not easy for Mr. and Mrs. Samuel Satterly. Worn out by child-bearing and the rigors of raising a large family under trying conditions, Eliza became ill and died in 1891. She was only forty-five years old.

Although devastated by the loss of his wife, Sam continued to labor in the Calumet and Hecla mines. But his health, too, was beginning to fail. All the years of hard labor, a chronic lung condition and several injuries took their toll and the proud Cornish miner was forced to retire. When he became too feeble to live alone, he moved to Minnesota to reside with Eveline, his eldest daughter. On October 9, 1916, Samuel Satterly died at age eighty years, five months and six days. The death certificate gave the cause of death as "old age" and noted that "he died suddenly while sitting in his chair." Way to go, Grandpa! And the same to me someday.

Lon Emerick

Methodist Church at Reunion time, Central

Lon Emerick

Goldenrod near Central

Lon Emerick

Mine ruins at Central

On this September evening, it is difficult to imagine a busy mining town here. The empty streets, the crumbled ruins of the old pump house, the huge piles of gray waste rock all create a somber mood. I stroll about searching for old home sites. Which one of these overgrown rock foundations supported the Satterly home? Is it that one over there with tansy and lilacs crowded close to a jumbled row of stones? It doesn't really matter, though, which house Eliza and Sam lived in—their spirits abide in all of Central.

I walk up a steep hill to the vast pile of rock and search for an overlooked fragment of copper or a small piece of greenstone to keep as a memento. Finding none, I select a flat stone for a seat and reflect on the old townsite spread out before me. I think I know these Cornish pioneers who lived, toiled, laughed and loved here so long ago. I have closed the circle about my ancestors and learned, yet again, that they live on in me. Remembering the poem I brought for just this moment, I unfold the small slip of paper and read:

My Kin

If you could see your ancestors
All standing in a row,
Would you be proud of them or not?
Or don't you really know?
Some strange discoveries are made
In climbing family trees,
And some of the ones you know,
Do not particularly please.
If you could see your ancestors
All standing in a row
There might be some among them
Whom you wouldn't care to know.
But there's another matter which
Requires a different view,
If you could see your ancestors,
Would they be proud of you?
(Author unknown)

Indeed, what would my kin think of this autumnal quest? Would they be proud of me? They say old miners never die, they just keep chiseling away. I think I can detect a faint clink of metal on rock—perhaps the answers I seek are somehow encoded in these muted clinks.

At the end of the classic film, *Jeremiah Johnson*, there is a scene that always makes me think of Central and my maternal ancestors. Jeremiah, played by Robert Redford, is camped comfortably in a winter setting when his old mountain-man mentor happens by. Impressed by the skills that Jeremiah has acquired since he saw him last, the mentor compliments Jeremiah on his achievements. Now, as I recall the lines from that movie scene, I imagine Great-great Grandfather Samuel Satterly as my own mentor:

> *"You have come far, Pilgrim."*
> *"Seems like far, Grandfather."*
> *"Were it worth the trouble, Lad?"*
> *"What? What trouble?"*

EPILOGUE

In Sam's Footsteps

T he pilgrimage was complete: I had gone back to Central and honored my Cornish forebears. Yet, there remained a vague unease, a lack of closure for my quest. After inspecting some old maps of the Keweenaw Peninsula, I knew what I had to do: I must follow Samuel Satterly's footsteps as he made his way to Central in 1860. I must walk to the old mining town from Eagle Harbor.

Once resolved to undertake the trek, I wanted to share the journey with another Cousin Jack. Would my friend Dean Premo like to join me on this jaunt through history? He would. And, an unexpected and delightful bonus, so would his family. My cup of Cornish joy spilled over the rim and warmed my soul.

And so it was, on a warm, sunny day in August, we assembled on the beautiful sandy beach in Eagle Harbor. Each of the participants was given a Cornish name: I, of course, was Samuel Satterly; Dean became cousin John Satterly; Bette was Eliza Chewidden; Evan became a young Cornish miner, Robert Penhale; Evan's friend, Emily, was Emily Jane Trezona; and Laurel was Sarah Rosemergy. One final hiker was Maizey, a yellow Lab, and she was herself: inquisitive, indefatigable and an artist of olfaction. We dipped St. Piran's banner in the waters of Lake Superior and marched out of town.

What a compelling and curious sight we made as, waving the Cornish black and white national flag, our troop of happy hikers headed south and west toward Central. Only a few cars passed by on this Sunday morning, but in each case they slowed and stared in wonder. One motorist was so astounded that he turned and drove past our procession several times.

Swiftly we passed Eliza Creek, Owl Creek and the old road leading to another abandoned mining town, Copper Falls. At the midpoint in the six-mile trek, we stopped and savored a Cornish treat, fresh saffron buns, and wondered if Samuel and his companions might have paused at this very spot to restore themselves. None of us latter-day re-enactors had much to say as we munched on the rolls but we all felt the pull of Cornish memories deep in the taste of the saffron.

Leaving the macadam highway, we turned on an old tote road that twisted through the dense forest. The woods are dark and deep and must have been quite a surprise to the young people from the moors and rocky headlands of Cornwall.

The narrow road rose steeply and, upon reaching the summit, we looked back at Lake Superior, the Blue Profound, framed by the deep green of lofty trees.

We were going to meet my wife, Lynn, at Central Lake. Lynn served our merry band as shuttle driver, and when we reached the old town, would take us back to the Premo vehicle. Maizey's magnificent nose led us through a narrow defile in the pines to where Lynn waited on a rock outcropping overlooking the small lake. The sun sparkled on the water and the small falls at the outlet added a note to the wind in the white pines.

The younger hikers needed little rest and restoration and soon all three of them were walking ahead of the adults. Looking at the talented and energetic trio saun-tering along in the dappled sunlight, a line from Bill Staines' song, "Child of Mine," one of *White Water*'s repertoire, came to mind: "They are tomorrow on the wing."

Central was drowsing in the midday warmth when we marched into the old town. We paused by miners' simple houses, many now restored for summer homes. A few of the original company houses are now year-round residences; we made sure to respect their privacy as we inspected crumbling mining structures, marveled at the restoration of the company agent's home, and then rested on the steps of the well-kept Methodist Church. We could sense the presence of the nineteenth centu-ry Cornish miners and their descendants. Leaving Central, we all felt a new and better connection to our ancestors who came here and built a life so long ago.*

---

*Laurel Premo prepared an initial draft of this epilogue.

Dean Premo

Laurel Premo does a Cornish jig on the Eagle Harbor beach

Lynn Emerick

The hikers rest on the Central church steps

CODA

Robert Yuill, former university professor, fresh water sailor and fellow saunterer, composed a song to honor my search for the past. What a poignant surprise it was when the *White Water* family band performed the public debut of "Back to Central" during a concert at the historic Calumet Theatre.

Back to Central

for Lon

R. Yuill 2001

To Central I've come back to see the	place that is a part of me, A simple place where
The land lies still there's no one here, the	town's returned to bear and deer. Grandfathers house has
From Cornwall did a miner roam and	struggled here to make a home. He worked to raise a
Oh can you hear his miner's pick be-	neath the ground where dark is thick; The rumble of those
His trace has vanished from the land. Where	is the spot he put his hand? Was all his toil
He's not on lists in halls of fame but	he was special just the same. His gifts were not in

hills divide And in that place my roots abide. For I'm
gone to dust And mining shafts have turned to rust.
family To build a life for them and me.
cars of ore And each day like the one before.
grief and pain a waste of effort made in vain?
things you see, His legacy was family.

coming home coming home, back where the mines took their toll, Yes I'm

coming home coming home back to the place of my soul.

157

BACK TO CENTRAL

R. Yuill 2001

To Central I've come back to see
The place that is a part of me,
A simple place where hills divide
And in that place my roots abide.

Chorus (after each verse)

For I'm coming home, coming home,
back where the mines took their toll,
Yes, I'm coming home, coming home,
back to the place of my soul.

The land lies still, there's no one here,
the town's returned to bear and deer.
Grandfather's house has gone to dust
And mining shafts have turned to rust.

From Cornwall did a miner roam
and struggled here to make a home.
He worked to raise a family
To build a life for them and me.

Oh can you hear his miner's pick
beneath the ground where dark is thick.
The rumble of those cars of ore
And each day like the one before.

His trace has vanished from the land.
Where is the spot he put his hand?
Was all his toil, grief and pain
a waste of effort made in vain?

He's not on lists in halls of fame
but he was special just the same.
His gifts were not in things you see.
His legacy was family.

ACKNOWLEDGMENTS

There would be no Going *Back to Central* without Richard Shelton and his wonderful book, *Going Back to Bisbee*.

Through his environmental consulting and the music magic of *White Water*, Dean Premo knows just about everyone in the Superior Peninsula. He was kind enough to direct me to several fascinating persons I met on my pilgrimage. The entire Premo family—Dean, Bette, Evan, Laurel and Maizey—was of great assistance and comfort during my sojourn.

Fellow saunterer, Richard Kierzek, was a bottomless reservoir of books and lore about mining, lumbering and almost any topic pertaining to the Upper Peninsula. He even gave me overnight visitation privileges with his personal "sticking Tommy."

The following individuals lent me their ears and their stories: Mabel LeMaire, Matt Obiden, Joe Sedlock, Ted and Shirley Kero, Mark Silver, Roy, Eila and Steve Koski, Wesley Ollila, John Perona, Charles Stetter, Tony Bausano, Peter and Patricia Van Pelt.

Nicole S. Walton, doyenne broadcaster and voice extraordinaire of Public Radio 90, scrutinized the entire manuscript with her usual efficiency and attention to detail.

Finally, without the assistance of Carol J. Watt and all the helpful librarians at the new, the magnificent Peter White Public Library in Marquette, I might still be lost among the shelves or yearning fruitlessly for the card catalogue.

Front cover photos: Lon Emerick
Back cover photos: Deep in the Copper Mine, Superior View Studio
Mine Ruins at Central, Lon Emerick